SELMA'S BLOODY SUNDAY

Witness to History

Peter Charles Hoffer and Williamjames Hull Hoffer, *Series Editors*

SELMA'S BLOODY SUNDAY

Protest, Voting Rights, and the Struggle for Racial Equality

ROBERT A. PRATT

UNIVERSITY OF GEORGIA, ATHENS

Johns Hopkins University Press | *Baltimore*

© 2017 Johns Hopkins University Press
All rights reserved. Published 2017
Printed in the United States of America on acid-free paper
9 8 7 6 5 4 3 2 1

Johns Hopkins University Press
2715 North Charles Street
Baltimore, Maryland 21218-4363
www.press.jhu.edu

Library of Congress Cataloging-in-Publication Data

Names: Pratt, Robert A., 1958– author.
Title: Selma's Bloody Sunday : protest, voting rights, and the struggle for
       racial equality / Robert A. Pratt.
Other titles: Witness to history (Baltimore, Md.)
Description: Baltimore : Johns Hopkins University Press, [2017] | ©2017 |
       Series: Witness to history | Includes bibliographical references and
       index.
Identifiers: LCCN 2016012790| ISBN 9781421421599 (hardcover : alk. paper)
       | ISBN 9781421421605 (pbk. : alk. paper) | ISBN 9781421421612
       (electronic) | ISBN 1421421593 (hardcover : alk. paper) |
       ISBN 1421421607 (pbk. : alk. paper) | ISBN 1421421615 (electronic)
Subjects: LCSH: African Americans—Civil rights—Alabama—Selma—
       History—20th century. | African Americans—Suffrage—Southern
       States—History—20th century. | Civil rights movements—United
       States—History—20th century.
Classification: LCC F334.S4 P73 2017 | DDC 323.1196/073076145—dc23
       LC record available at http://lccn.loc.gov/2016012790

A catalog record for this book is available from the British Library.

*Special discounts are available for bulk purchases of this book. For
more information, please contact Special Sales at 410-516-6936 or
specialsales@press.jhu.edu.*

Johns Hopkins University Press uses environmentally friendly book
materials, including recycled text paper that is composed of at least
30 percent post-consumer waste, whenever possible.

My memory stammers but my soul is a witness.
—James Baldwin, *The Evidence of Things Not Seen*

To all of the "witnesses" of Bloody Sunday, whose courage and determination helped to advance the cause of liberty and justice for all

And to Paul M. Gaston, my mentor and friend

CONTENTS

SELMA'S BLOODY SUNDAY

Prologue

ON SUNDAY AFTERNOON, MARCH 7, 1965, roughly six hundred marchers set out from Brown Chapel A.M.E. Church in a double-file column. Leading the marchers were Hosea Williams of the Southern Christian Leadership Conference (SCLC) and John Lewis of the Student Nonviolent Coordinating Committee (SNCC). The marchers headed down Sylvan Street from the church and turned right on Water Street. As the marchers remember it, there was no singing, no shouting—just the sound of their own heartbeats and the rhythm of marching feet. Upon reaching Broad Street they turned left and began their ascension across the towering arch referred to as the Edmund Pettus Bridge that spanned the Alabama River. The marchers were expecting resistance at some point, but to their surprise there were no police in sight—only a group of white men, gathered in front of the *Selma Times-Journal* newspaper building. They had hard hats on their heads and clubs in their hands. Some of them had smirks on their faces, but none said a word.

"When we reached the crest of the bridge," recalls John Lewis, "I stopped dead still. So did Hosea. There, facing us at the bottom of the other side, stood a sea of blue-helmeted, blue-uniformed Alabama state troopers, line after line of them, dozens of battle-ready lawmen stretched from one side of

On "Bloody Sunday," March 7, 1965, hundreds of marchers tried to cross the Edmund Pettus Bridge on the highway from Selma to Montgomery, the state capital, where they planned to demonstrate on behalf of their voting rights. The marchers ran into a small army of state troopers, who brutally attacked them. John Lewis, chairman of SNCC (wearing the light trench coat), who led the march along with Hosea Williams of SCLC, suffered a beating that left him with a fractured skull. The sheer magnitude of the violence shocked the nation. Prints and Photographs Division, Library of Congress

U.S. Highway 80 to the other. Behind them were several dozen more armed men—Sheriff Clark's posse—some on horseback, all wearing khaki clothing, many carrying clubs the size of baseball bats."[1] On the side of the highway was a crowd of about a hundred or so whites, some jeering and laughing and waving Confederate flags. Beyond them, watching at a safe distance, was a group of about fifty blacks. Reporters and their camera crews had been grouped together in front of a car dealership behind the troopers' line, and several of the troopers were positioned near them to make sure that none of them ventured from their position.

As the marchers approached the far side of the bridge, Major John Cloud ordered them to turn back. "This is an unlawful assembly," he said. "Your march is not conducive to the public safety. You are ordered to disperse; go back to your church or to your homes. This march will not continue. You have two minutes . . ."[2]

The brutality and horror that was about to unfold at the foot of the Edmund Pettus Bridge—a day that would come to be known as "Bloody Sunday"—would become one of the pivotal moments of the civil rights movement and would be etched indelibly into the memories of those who witnessed and endured it. The civil rights movement had been responsible for some significant changes in the ways that white Americans viewed African Americans; for decades, perhaps centuries, whites had taken for granted black people's acceptance of their second-class status. But by 1965, black Americans' dissatisfaction with the racial status quo was becoming increasingly apparent, as too was their willingness to confront the system of rigid segregation and racial discrimination that had served as the underpinning of a society based on white supremacy. The United States Supreme Court's 1954 unanimous ruling in *Brown v. Board of Education* had struck at segregation in public education, and ten years later the 1964 Civil Rights Act, aimed at eliminating once and for all the remaining vestiges of racial discrimination in American life, had been passed into law by the Congress and signed by President Lyndon B. Johnson. Yet despite these judicial and legislative milestones, the most basic and fundamental right of citizenship—the right to vote—remained out of reach for the masses of African Americans residing in the states of the former Confederacy.

What follows is the story of a civil rights campaign that unfolded in Selma, Alabama, in the spring of 1965, almost one hundred years to the day that the nation ended its bloody Civil War that had been fought over black slavery. But the story of Selma is about much more than African Americans protesting for the right to vote. This is a story about the triumph of black and white protest over white resistance, the fulfillment of the promise of the Fifteenth Amendment ratified in 1870, the freedom guaranteed to all Americans by the Declaration of Independence and the U.S. Constitution, and the countless lives lost in the process of gaining that freedom. What started in Selma as a bloody conflict over who should have access to the ballot would end with a triumphant march to Montgomery—the former "Cradle of the Confederacy"—that would begin a political transformation and realignment that would have far-reaching implications for decades to come. The election of the nation's first African-American president in 2008 perhaps reflected the apex of black political power. But that election also revealed an interesting paradox: an increase in black electoral participation and a rapidly changing political landscape prompted white conservatives to resort to a new campaign of voter restrictions in order to preserve Republican Party domination. It would appear that the lessons of Selma have yet to be learned.

1

Slow March toward Freedom

Slavery is not abolished until the black man has the right to vote.

—Frederick Douglass, 1865

ON APRIL 9, 1865, exactly a century before the bloody confrontation in Selma, Confederate general Robert E. Lee had surrendered to Union general Ulysses S. Grant at Appomattox Courthouse in Virginia, ending the four bloodiest years in American history. While Confederate leaders claimed that the war was about maintaining the "Southern way of life" and states' rights, and President Lincoln never wavered in his position that the war was being fought to "preserve the Union," the issues of slavery and race were always at the center of the conflict between North and South. Lincoln's Emancipation Proclamation, issued on January 1, 1863, was a powerful symbol, but it would not be until the ratification of the Thirteenth Amendment in 1865 that slavery would finally be abolished. The former slaves, now referred to as freedmen, would begin to make the gradual transition from slavery to freedom and in the process seek to find their place in a society that had long considered blacks to be subhuman, whether they were slave or free. Indeed, the Supreme Court's ruling in *Dred Scott v. Sandford* in 1857 was defined in terms of race, not slave status, when Chief Justice Roger B. Taney wrote that

"Neither the class of persons who had been imported as slaves, nor their descendants, whether they had become free or not, were then acknowledged as a part of the people . . . [and that they are] so far inferior, that they had no rights which the white man was bound to respect."[1]

When the Civil War ended, roughly four million people of African descent who had previously been enslaved were suddenly free. But their status as free people was far from certain. President Lincoln, the "Great Emancipator," was now dead at the hands of John Wilkes Booth, and Lincoln's successor, Andrew Johnson, was no friend to blacks. Lincoln's body was barely cold before Johnson began making overtures to the former Confederates, which included issuing more than 13,500 pardons during the summer of 1865. As a result of those pardons, former Confederates regained the land that they had forfeited during the war years—land that thousands of African Americans had been working on with the expectation that eventually that land would be theirs.[2] With that land being returned to their former slave masters, blacks had little choice but to return to those same plantations, this time not as slaves but as sharecroppers, an economic arrangement that threw them into perennial indebtedness, escape from which was all but impossible. Despite the passage of the Thirteenth Amendment, which abolished slavery, the rise of sharecropping, along with the convict-lease system (which has been referred to as slavery by another name), meant that economic prospects for African Americans would be dim for the remainder of the nineteenth and well into the twentieth century.[3]

Without land to provide former slaves with economic independence, the right to vote became all the more important. The issue of black suffrage had been debated before the Civil War came to an end. While some white abolitionists believed their work was accomplished with the ratification of the Thirteenth Amendment, other black and white abolitionists argued that black men's enfranchisement was the only way to protect their freedom. On this matter, the black abolitionist Frederick Douglass was direct and to the point: "Slavery is not abolished until the black man has the right to vote."[4] Northern whites were only slightly more receptive to the idea of black men voting than their southern counterparts, as virtually all of the northern states prevented black men from voting. Prior to the ratification of the Fourteenth and Fifteenth Amendments, only in New England could black men vote or hold office.

The freedmen clearly understood that their freedom would be meaningless without access to the ballot. Similarly, congressional Republicans knew that unless the freedmen (who would presumably vote Republican) were enfranchised, the states of the former Confederacy would be governed once again by the same white Democrats who had voted for secession from the Union. No doubt, President Lincoln had understood this as well. But when he had suggested limited suffrage for black men in the newly readmitted state of Louisiana in 1864, that state's all-white legislature rejected the idea. If Lincoln's proposal of limited suffrage for black men—by which he meant only those who were educated or who had fought for the Union—could be rejected, then there was little chance that southern whites would ever voluntarily accept the idea of universal black suffrage.

Andrew Johnson continued Lincoln's lenient policies toward former Confederates. Johnson quickly restored civilian governments in the southern states, issued proclamations of amnesty for thousands of former Confederates, and showed no interest whatsoever in protecting the rights of the freedmen. Soon thereafter, the southern states passed what became known as the "Black Codes," a series of laws aimed at restricting the rights of the former slaves. By late 1865, the reorganized southern states were holding elections and former Confederates were returning to Congress to reclaim their seats as if the war had never happened. These actions infuriated most congressional Republicans, especially the "radical" Republicans, so named because of their liberal attitudes toward the freedmen. The struggle between President Johnson and Congress escalated in early 1866 when Congress passed two bills over Johnson's veto—the reauthorization and expansion of the Freedmen's Bureau and the Civil Rights Act of 1866.

Established in March 1865, the Freedmen's Bureau aimed to help the freedmen make their transition from slavery to freedom by providing them with economic and educational assistance. Because the freedmen had reported numerous cases of abuses by the former Confederates, Congress extended the life and expanded the powers of the Bureau in 1866, authorizing it to establish military commissions to hear cases of civil rights abuses. To further protect the rights of freed people, Congress passed the Civil Rights Act of 1866, which defined U.S. citizenship for the first time and affirmed that all citizens were entitled to basic civil rights. When Johnson raised concerns about the constitutionality of the civil rights bill (in light of the Supreme Court's ruling in *Dred Scott* that blacks were not citizens), Congress proposed the Fourteenth Amendment, which would guarantee citizenship rights for the freedmen.

Ratified in 1868, this amendment guaranteed "equal protection of the laws" to all citizens. Declaring that "all persons born or naturalized in the United States" are "citizens of the United States and of the State wherein they reside," it reversed the *Dred Scott* decision of 1857. The bill was then sent to the states (including the southern states) for ratification.

Outmaneuvered by congressional Republicans, Johnson embarked upon an unprecedented speaking tour, urging the former Confederates not to ratify the Fourteenth Amendment. Having grown weary of southern intransigence and President Johnson's obstinacy, congressional Republicans took control of Reconstruction away from Johnson in 1867. On March 2, 1867, Congress passed the Reconstruction Act of 1867, which dissolved state governments in the former Confederacy (except for Tennessee, which had voted to ratify the Fourteenth Amendment) and divided the South into five military districts subject to martial law. To reenter the Union, a state was required to call a constitutional convention, the delegates for which would be elected by universal male suffrage (including black men over the age of twenty-one and excluding white Confederate leaders); to write a new constitution that guaranteed black male suffrage; and to ratify the Fourteenth Amendment.

Since many former Confederates were ineligible to vote in elections for delegates to state constitutional conventions, and up to 30 percent of whites refused to participate in elections in which black men could vote, in some southern states more blacks than whites were voting. Of the more than 1,000 delegates elected to write new state constitutions, 268 were black. In South Carolina and Louisiana, blacks were in the majority. Black men throughout the former Confederate states and the District of Columbia voted and held office for the first time, all as Republicans. The Union Army oversaw the process of registering 735,000 black and 635,000 white men. Five states—Mississippi, South Carolina, Louisiana, Alabama, and Florida—had black electoral majorities.[5]

In a historic first, seven African Americans were elected to the Forty-First and Forty-Second Congresses. Between 1869 and 1901 twenty-two blacks served in Congress—two in the U.S. Senate and twenty in the House of Representatives. Every state of the former Confederacy had at least one African American representative in Congress. Both black senators represented the state of Mississippi. In a twist of irony, Hiram Revels, who had been born free, was chosen by the Mississippi legislature to fill the unexpired senate term of former Confederate president Jefferson Davis. His term in the Senate lasted for only one year. Mississippi's other U.S. senator, Blanche K. Bruce, was a former slave who served one six-year term.

More than a few blacks achieved high political office in various state governments. Like their congressional counterparts, these officeholders were all Republicans. In Louisiana, Mississippi, and South Carolina, blacks served as lieutenant governors. In Louisiana, P. B. S. Pinchback served as acting governor for forty-three days. All across the South, more than six hundred blacks served in state legislatures. During this period of what came to be known as "Black Reconstruction" (so named because of the unprecedented African American involvement in the political process) some 2,000 blacks served as officeholders at the various levels of government in the states of the former Confederacy. Although slightly more than half of them had been slaves, many of them were now literate, fair-minded, and committed as government officials. They served as superintendents of education, sheriffs, police officers, city councilmen, tax collectors, registrars, county commissioners, and postmasters. In a political era marked by graft and corruption, black politicians proved to be more ethical than their white counterparts. And, with but few exceptions, fears of southern whites that black lawmakers would be vindictive and bent on retribution against their former masters did not materialize. Wherever they served, they sought to balance the interests of black and white southerners and, more often than not, erred on the side of leniency and reconciliation.

It is important to note that despite this political revolution of sorts that was occurring in the states of the former Confederacy, white southern resistance to black electoral participation continued unabated. Five of the first twenty blacks elected to the House of Representatives were denied their seats, and ten others had their terms interrupted or delayed. The charges against these individuals were frivolous and frequently fabricated, often having to do with alleged voting irregularities. James Lewis, John Willis Menard, and Pinchney B. S. Pinchback, all from Louisiana, were charged with voter fraud by whites who themselves were involved in ballot box tampering. Whites were successful in challenging the credentials of these three elected Louisiana representatives, and they were never seated in the House.[6]

Blacks who had been elected to the state legislatures often fared no better. What southern whites referred to contemptuously as the "era of Negro rule" and domination never existed. At no point in any part of the Reconstructed South did black men rule. In the state legislatures of 1867, black men held the majority only in South Carolina's lower house, and there only briefly; whites always controlled the South Carolina senate. Elsewhere, black officeholders experienced serious difficulties taking and holding office. In Georgia, for instance, white legislators prevented black elected lawmakers from taking their seats (which resulted in Georgia being barred from the Union until 1870).

Despite the challenges they faced in their efforts to vote and to hold office, African Americans viewed the right to vote as the most important of all civil rights and the one on which all the others depended. To guarantee this right to future generations, the overwhelmingly Republican U.S. Congress proposed the Fifteenth Amendment in 1869, and it was ratified the next year. It declared, "The right of citizens of the United States to vote shall not be denied or abridged by the United States or by any State on account of race, color, or previous condition of servitude." With this amendment, many believed that the federal government's responsibility to the former slaves had been fulfilled. But if northern whites believed that the Fifteenth Amendment completed Reconstruction, southern whites remained defiant, believing that black political involvement was a strange perversion of civilization. For them, a world in which black men were voting and holding political office while white men were disenfranchised was a world that had been turned upside down. Sensing that the federal government's support of the freedmen was waning, white southerners began planning a counterrevolution that would "redeem" the South by restoring white "home rule." And if they could not achieve this by corrupting the political process, they meant to do so through violence and bloodshed.

By 1870 all of the former Confederate states had been readmitted to the Union, but the seeds of "redemption" had been sown in the 1860s, and by the end of the decade had begun to bear fruit. Long before the official end of Reconstruction in 1877 (delayed as a result of the disputed presidential election of 1876), white terror throughout the South had effectively forced blacks out of political office and served as an ever-present reminder of the fate that could befall any black man who dared to go to the polls. The Ku Klux Klan, founded in Tennessee in 1865, was clearly the best-known white terrorist organization; but there were others, such as the White Brotherhood and the Knights of the White Camelia. Often referred to as night riders because they carried out their acts of violence under cover of darkness, members of these organizations usually wore white robes and hoods to conceal their identity. Membership in these white supremacist organizations was not restricted to any particular social or economic class, as whites from all segments of society could be found among their ranks.

Much of the violence directed toward African Americans was motivated by a combination of outright racial animosity and white southerners' desire to eliminate blacks from the electorate, which was the first step in the process to overthrow Republican governments and return white supremacists to power in the South. In Colfax, Louisiana, a group of white Democrats, armed with rifles and cannon, overpowered Republican freedmen and the black state militia who were trying to maintain Republican control of the town. On Easter Sunday, April 13, 1873, more than 280 blacks were killed in the bloodiest racial massacre of that era. Most of the freedmen were killed after they had already surrendered, and at least 50 were killed later that night after having been held as prisoners for several hours. A similar attack occurred in 1876 in Hamburg, South Carolina, where skirmishes between black militiamen and local whites escalated into violence. Local whites, offended by the sight of black men in uniform, demanded that the black militiamen surrender their weapons following a dispute over free passage on a public road. The blacks refused, and later that evening hundreds of white men gathered and began an assault on the black militiamen, who took refuge in their armory. Six black men died at the hands of the white mob. And in 1898 in Wilmington, North Carolina, whites rigged the local election that resulted in every black office-holder being turned out of office. Not content to wait until the regular change of office, white Democratic Party insurgents overthrew the legitimately elected local government. Originally described as a riot, but what is today more accurately considered a coup d'état, a mob of more than two thousand white men attacked the only black newspaper in the state, destroyed property in black neighborhoods, and physically assaulted hundreds of black residents. Estimates of the number of blacks killed in Wilmington range from fifteen to more than sixty. Despite appeals from white and black Wilmington residents for federal intervention, President William McKinley refused to act. Events such as these clearly demonstrated the limits of armed black self-defense; even when blacks were willing to fight back, they were usually outnumbered and outgunned. These events also demonstrated the lengths to which whites were willing to go in order to regain political power as well as the reluctance of the federal government to intervene on the side of the freedmen.

As white opposition movements proceeded differently in each state, Reconstruction lasted different lengths of time in the various southern states.

In all of the former Confederate states except South Carolina, Florida, Louisiana, and Mississippi, Reconstruction had ended by the early 1870s, and white Democrats had regained power through either political shenanigans or intimidation and violence. Further, with the deaths of Thaddeus Stevens of Pennsylvania in 1868 and Charles Sumner of Massachusetts in 1874, the freedmen had lost their staunchest political allies, and increasing numbers of Republicans had grown weary of what they referred to as the "Negro Problem," believing they had done all they could on behalf of the former slaves. In one of its last attempts to protect the rights of the freedmen, Congress passed two Force Acts, in 1870 and 1871, to protect the civil rights of blacks as defined in the Fourteenth and Fifteenth Amendments. Federal troops rather than state militias were authorized to rein in white terror organizations, and those who conspired to deprive blacks of their civil rights were tried in federal rather than state and local courts. But this was merely a temporary fix, and even then an imperfect one. When federal charges were brought against several members of the white mob that had slaughtered blacks in the Colfax Massacre, the U.S. Supreme Court overturned the white men's convictions, ruling that the "Due Process Clause" and the "Equal Protection Clause" of the Fourteenth Amendment only applies to state action, not individual citizens. Put another way, the Supreme Court's position in *United States v. Cruikshank* (1876) was that the Fourteenth Amendment could be used to prevent *state governments* from murdering African Americans, but could not be used to prevent *white individuals* from murdering them. By the time the last of the federal troops were removed from the South in 1877 (a concession made by Republicans to southern Democrats in exchange for southern acceptance of a Rutherford B. Hayes presidency) blacks were left to fend for themselves.[7] The reconciliation of North and South for economic gain was far more important to white northerners than any lingering concerns they may have had for black folk.

Throughout the remainder of the nineteenth century, the U.S. Supreme Court, as it had done in *Cruikshank*, would undermine the few legal protections that Congress had sought to bestow upon African Americans. Although the Fourteenth Amendment had been written to confer citizenship upon African Americans, in the *Slaughterhouse* cases of 1873 the Supreme Court increasingly reinterpreted "persons" to mean corporations rather than black people; hence, the Fourteenth Amendment was used to protect corporations from regulation, not to protect the rights of blacks. In *United States v. Reese*

(1876), the first voting rights case to be brought before the Supreme Court under the Fifteenth Amendment, the court held that the Fifteenth Amendment did not grant to African Americans the right to vote, but merely prohibited their exclusion on the basis of race. This blueprint for disenfranchisement would be implemented by one southern state after another and would effectively remove blacks from the voting rolls for nearly a century.

In 1890 Mississippi became the first of the former Confederate states to disenfranchise black men by revising its state constitution. The Mississippi Constitutional Convention of 1890 passed an amendment, often referred to as "The Mississippi Plan for Disenfranchisement," that imposed a poll tax of $2; excluded voters convicted of bribery, burglary, theft, arson, perjury, murder, or bigamy; and also barred anyone who could not read any section of the state constitution, understand it when read, or give a reasonable interpretation of it (to the satisfaction of the white registrar). As Mississippi state representative James K. Vardaman put it, "The Mississippi Convention was held for no other purpose than to eliminate the nigger from voting."[8] In 1895 South Carolina followed with similar restrictions, including a requirement that a voter own property worth at least three hundred dollars. In addition, South Carolina required that special ballots and boxes be placed in every polling place for each office on the ballot, and that voters must put their ballots in the correct boxes in order for their votes to be counted. Of all the schemes designed to discourage blacks from voting, the poll tax was one of the most effective. Anyone wanting to vote had to pay the tax months before the election, and then retain the receipt as proof of having paid. The tax was also cumulative, so that an individual would have to prove that he had paid the tax every year since turning twenty-one; if not, he would have to pay previous years' taxes to become current. As a consequence, hundreds of thousands of black men (and tens of thousands of white men) were discouraged from voting. Running a close second to the poll tax in effectiveness was the literacy test, also known as the "understanding clause." A South Carolina delegate to his state's convention said of the "understanding clause": "My 'understanding' is that this will disenfranchise every negro."[9]

By 1910 blacks had been disenfranchised by constitutional amendments in Arkansas, Louisiana, Tennessee, Florida, North Carolina, Alabama, Virginia, Georgia, Texas, and Oklahoma. In addition to poll taxes and literacy tests, these states used property and residency requirements, fraud, trickery, and subterfuge, and when all else failed, raw terror. To minimize the impact that these schemes would have on poor whites who were also disenfranchised by the thousands, states created a "grandfather clause" that would allow a man to vote if his father or grandfather had voted prior to January 1, 1867. Most states that had permitted free people of color to vote in the early decades of the nineteenth century had rescinded that right before 1840. Thus, even African Americans who might have descended from families that were free before the Civil War could not get an exemption from literacy tests or other restrictive measures.

The impact that these disenfranchisement schemes had on African Americans was quick and devastating. In 1896 there were roughly 121,000 eligible black voters in Alabama; by 1900 that number had been reduced to 3,742. In Louisiana there were 130,334 eligible black voters in 1896; within four years there were only 5,320 blacks on the rolls. By 1910 only 730 blacks were registered; in 27 of the state's 60 parishes not a single black voter was registered, and in 9 parishes only one black voter was registered. In Mississippi, the number of black qualified voters was reduced from 135,000 to virtually none.

In two court cases decided at the end of the century, the U.S. Supreme Court upheld the constitutionality of these disenfranchisement schemes. In *Mills v. Green* (1895) and *Williams v. Mississippi* (1898) the court ruled against the black men who had sued their states for racist disenfranchisement. In essence, the court's rationale was that because race or color was not specifically mentioned in any of these new voting requirements, they did not violate the Fifteenth Amendment. These rulings, taken together, were as effective as any lynch mob in keeping African Americans away from the polls. As a result of the calculated ingenuity of white southern legislators and the cold indifference of Supreme Court justices, the promise of the Fifteenth Amendment would remain unfulfilled as the nineteenth century drew to a close.

As African Americans disappeared from the voting rolls, so too did African American lawmakers vanish from state legislatures and Congress. George H. White of North Carolina, who took his seat in 1897, would be the last black to serve in Congress for generations. In his final address to Congress on January 29, 1901, he said: "This, Mr. Chairman, is perhaps the Negroes' temporary farewell to the American Congress. But let me say, phoenix-like, he will rise up someday and come again. These parting words are in behalf of an outraged, heartbroken, bruised and bleeding people, but God fearing people, faithful, industrious, loyal people . . . full of potential."[10]

At the turn of the twentieth century, African Americans were no longer a presence in southern politics. Yet despite that, southern states continued to benefit from disproportionate representation in Congress, because congressional representation is based on a state's *total* population rather than its actual *voting* population. In a strange twist of irony, this meant that the South's heavy black population empowered racist southern politicians to continue their discriminatory practices. For example, Kansas, with a total voting population of 425,641, had eight congressional representatives, while Louisiana, with a total voting population of 44,794, also had eight. South Carolina, with a total voting population of only 25,433, had seven representatives (South Carolina's total population was majority black). Iowa and Minnesota, with total votes of 316,377 and 299,127, respectively, each had ten representatives; but so too did Alabama, which had a total vote of only 62,345. California, with a total voting population of 644,790, had eleven representatives, while Georgia, with a total vote of 59,196, had twelve. Northern lawmakers were very much aware of this representational imbalance, and from 1896 to 1900 the House of Representatives had acted in over thirty cases to set aside election results from southern states because the House Elections Committee had concluded that "black voters had been excluded due to fraud, violence, or intimidation." Congressman Edgar D. Crumpacker of Indiana proposed stripping southern states of seats to reflect the number of people they had disenfranchised. But the power of the southern Democratic bloc was too strong, and his proposal never gained any traction.[11]

African Americans continued to mount legal challenges to their disenfranchisement, and the federal courts continued to rule against them. Jackson W. Giles, a literate African American who had been voting in Alabama from 1871 to 1901, found himself disenfranchised under the state's new constitution. One of the new provisions held that any person registered before January 1, 1903 (as most whites were) would thereafter be registered for life; but any person not registered at that time (as most blacks were not) would have to overcome a number of hurdles to be allowed to register. Among those hurdles was a test of the potential registrant's understanding of the duties and obligations of citizenship. This test was administered by white election officials, who conducted it in a subjective manner that resulted in most whites being approved to register and most blacks being rejected from registering. Giles filed suit on behalf of more than five thousand black citizens of Montgomery, Alabama, and himself in seeking to have the federal courts require the state to register them as voters. In the case of *Giles v. Harris* (1903), the U.S. Supreme

Court upheld Alabama's voter registration restrictions. The decision, written by Oliver Wendell Holmes, who had suffered three wounds as a Union officer, declared that the provisions did not target blacks specifically and thus did not deprive them of their rights. Not even *he* would come to the aid of a frustrated black petitioner. Booker T. Washington, who by this time was Alabama's most famous black citizen and who had become best known for his accommodationist views regarding racial equality, worked quietly behind the scenes to raise funds for this and other lawsuits challenging segregation and disenfranchisement.

With the founding of the National Association for the Advancement of Colored People (NAACP) in 1909, legal challenges to racial segregation and disenfranchisement intensified. Unlike the many other civil rights organizations that would follow in later decades, the NAACP was committed to challenging various forms of discrimination through the legal process. When the U.S. Supreme Court in 1915 overturned Oklahoma's "grandfather clause" in the case of *United States v. Guinn*, the NAACP filed its first amicus brief. This decision affected similar provisions in the constitutions of other southern states including Alabama, Georgia, Louisiana, North Carolina, and Virginia. Since the main purpose of the grandfather clause had been to provide a loophole for poor whites who would have otherwise been disqualified from voting under the same restrictions that disqualified blacks, the immediate impact of the decision was to disqualify tens of thousands of southern whites. In the ensuing decades, however, southern state legislatures would gradually expand voting opportunities for poor whites while finding ever more creative ways of denying such opportunities to blacks. For example, as soon as the Supreme Court struck down Oklahoma's grandfather clause, the state legislature quickly passed a new law further restricting voter registration. The mere wording of this new statute made its discriminatory intent evident. The new law provided that "all persons, except those who voted in 1914, who were qualified to vote in 1916 but who failed to register between April 30 and May 11, 1916, with some exceptions for sick and absent persons who were given an additional brief period to register, would be perpetually disenfranchised."[12]

From the 1860s to the 1960s, the Democratic Party dominated southern politics. Such was the party's stronghold in the South during these years that winning the Democratic primary election was tantamount to winning the regular election, since the Republican Party—still viewed as the party of the Union and Abraham Lincoln—was virtually nonexistent in the South. This political reality meant that the only election that mattered was the one that occurred within the Democratic Party. Beginning in the 1920s southern states began using the *white primary* as a way of locking blacks out of the electoral process. By claiming to be a *private* club that had the right to determine its own membership, the Democratic Party in many southern states restricted membership to whites only, while denying it to blacks. Southern state legislatures acted as accomplices, closing the primaries to everyone except party members, which, according to the federal courts, was perfectly legal. The U.S. Supreme Court had ruled in 1921, in *Newberry v. United States*, that political parties were private organizations and were not part of the government election apparatus. And since political parties were private organizations, African Americans' disenfranchisement was not the result of official state action that would have triggered judicial review under the Fourteenth Amendment's Equal Protection Clause.

The passage of the Nineteenth Amendment in 1920, which extended the franchise to women, combined with the heroic efforts of black army veterans returning from World War I, prompted African Americans to accelerate their demands for voting rights. In a series of legal challenges to the white primary beginning in the late 1920s, the Supreme Court finally began to adopt the position that primaries were indeed part of a state's political machinery. In *Nixon v. Herndon* (1927) the court struck down a 1923 Texas law that prohibited blacks from voting in the Texas Democratic Party primary; and, in the landmark decision *Smith v. Allwright* in 1944 the court ruled that the white primary in Texas (and by extension, all other states) violated the Fifteenth Amendment's prohibition of voting discrimination based on race. Not to be outdone, Texas Democrats established a "private association" from which African Americans were excluded. The members of that association then held "preprimary" elections to select candidates for the Democratic primaries. But in *Terry v. Adams* (1953) the Supreme Court declared that the preprimary was also unconstitutional.

Although some African Americans did begin to register to vote after the end of the all-white primaries, the vast majority of blacks remained locked out of the electoral process, as southern states continued to rely on other discriminatory practices, such as poll taxes and literacy tests, to keep the number of black voters as low as possible. With the exception of Texas and Arkansas, all of the former Confederate states had written literacy tests for voting into their constitutions. Since blacks suffered the most from a lack of schooling, they obviously bore the heaviest burden of proving their literacy—which would have been difficult even if the tests had been administered fairly. In the South, however, white registrars were a law unto themselves and implemented the rules as they saw fit. Registrars had wide latitude in determining who was and who was not eligible to vote, and they had the power to routinely disqualify African Americans for virtually any reason they could conceive of. In Birmingham, Alabama, for instance, blacks experienced difficulty in answering "What is the Constitution made of?" and "How does the government of the United States operate?" Even when black college students and teachers could respond correctly, local registrars and clerks failed them on minor points. One educator failed because she omitted the word "more" in reciting the preamble to the Constitution. Of course, white applicants did not have to clear such hurdles.[13]

Clerks were able to discourage voter registration even without administering any examinations. Working at a snail's pace, they deliberately kept blacks standing in long lines and refused to provide any assistance in filling out the necessary forms. Then at the designated closing time, registrars abruptly closed the office, regardless of how many people were waiting in line. In Alabama, boards used a voucher system that required potential black registrants to bring in two white men who could identify them. Although blacks who had been disqualified had thirty days to appeal their denial, local boards easily nullified this option by waiting more than a month to notify a person that he did not meet the qualifications. As in most of the states of the Deep South, Alabama had deliberately designed its voter registration system to prevent blacks from voting. These various schemes, ruses, and subterfuges, along with the all-white primary, effectively reduced the number of eligible black voters in Alabama from roughly 121,000 in 1896 to 6,000 in 1947.[14]

The Supreme Court's ruling in *Smith v. Allwright* buoyed the hopes and aspirations of blacks across the South, and many of them, with the additional prompting of various voters leagues being formed throughout the South, began to register to vote for the first time. The message of the Progressive Voters League appealed especially to African American veterans returning from the fight in World War II. Having fought against Nazism and Fascism in Europe and having witnessed firsthand the horrors of the Jewish concentration camps, black soldiers had waged a "Double-V" campaign (victory abroad against Hitler and victory at home against racism). NAACP assistant secretary Roy Wilkins remarked that for black soldiers who had dodged enemy fire in Europe "bullets or threats of bullets are not likely to cause them to bow and scrape once they are home."[15] In the eastern Mississippi town of Decatur, black army veteran Medgar Evers had managed to register and looked forward to voting against Theodore Bilbo, the state's best-known racist demagogue. But on the night before the election, a group of whites paid Evers's father a visit and warned him to keep his son away from the polls. Despite the threat, Evers and four other black veterans showed up the next day at the polling place—but they did not vote, as several white men brandishing pistols turned them away. Encounters like this were repeated all across the South and made it clear to black veterans that their attempts to claim victory at home would be fraught with just as much danger as had been their efforts to secure it abroad.

Many white southern politicians, incensed by the court's ruling to end the white primaries, redoubled their efforts to deny African Americans the vote, vowing to do so by any means necessary, legal or extralegal. During his 1946 campaign for re-nomination to the senate in Mississippi, Theodore Bilbo, a member of the Ku Klux Klan whose name had become synonymous with white supremacy, brazenly counseled Mississippi's registrars to use their discretionary powers to prevent blacks from registering to vote. He told a large and lively crowd that if "there is a single man or woman serving . . . who cannot think up questions enough to disqualify undesirables then write Bilbo or any good lawyer, and there are a hundred good questions which can be furnished." And for any of those "undesirables" who managed to register, Bilbo had another idea. He told the crowd, "But you know . . . the best way to keep the nigger from voting. You do it the night before the election. I don't have to tell you any more than that. Red-blooded men know what I mean." The audience went wild.[16]

Taking a page from the Bilbo handbook as he sought the 1946 Georgia gubernatorial nomination, Eugene Talmadge warned that "wise Negroes will stay away from the white man's ballot boxes."[17] As events unfolded, it was clear that Talmadge's warning was to be taken seriously. Maceo Snipes had served in the Pacific during World War II and had returned home to make history by becoming the first African American to vote in Taylor County, Georgia. But on July 18, 1946, a day after he voted in the Georgia Democratic primary, the 37-year-old army veteran was shot in the back by four white men and collapsed in the doorway of his home. He died two days later. In Wrightsville, Georgia, Klansmen had marched through the streets warning that "blood would flow" if blacks voted in the upcoming election. On September 8, two white brothers warned black army veteran Isaac Nixon against voting. Disregarding their advice he voted shortly after dawn, and was murdered before sunset. As he lay dying, he revealed the names of his assailants. Two months later, an all-white jury acquitted the two brothers.

Blacks who dared to challenge the system by voting clearly understood the risks involved. But those who went beyond voting and actively worked to expand the black electorate by encouraging African Americans to register and vote were more visible targets, and they rarely escaped with just a warning or a beating. In June 1950, Alvin Jones, a black college instructor educated in the North, tried to assist a group of black registrants in Louisiana. A white clerk informed Jones and the group that "Niggers can't register here," and when Jones and the others refused to leave, a group of whites brutally beat him and his companions inside the courthouse. Jones later died from his injuries. In Brevard County, Florida, a black NAACP activist named Harry T. Moore, president of the state's Conference of Branches, had formed the Florida Progressive Voters League. As a result of Moore's efforts, the number of African American voters had increased statewide from 5 percent of those eligible to 31 percent. From 1944 to 1950 Moore and the Progressive Voters League had succeeded in registering 116,000 black voters, twice as many as were registered in any other southern state. Moore's efforts to register black voters, as well as his broader civil rights activism, had made him a target of the local Ku Klux Klan. On Christmas night, 1951, dynamite exploded under Moore's house, killing him instantly. His wife, Harriette, died eight days later. Following an investigation, NAACP executive secretary Walter White revealed that some whites had "expressed alarm over the growth of Negro voting strength in Florida," and that "they thought too many Negroes were getting 'funny ideas' like Harry T. Moore." The killers were never brought to trial.[18]

The short-term impact of the Supreme Court's 1954 landmark *Brown v. Board of Education* decision on black voting is somewhat mixed. While there is little doubt that the court's decision ending segregation in public education sent a powerful message to African Americans across the nation that the high court was becoming more sympathetic to black demands for racial justice, the decision resonated just as profoundly with many whites, but for a totally different reason. Many observers believed that the *Brown* decision made some southern whites more sensitive to what they may have perceived as Negro assertiveness, thereby increasing racial tensions exponentially. Every initiative undertaken by African Americans to improve their lot was countered by intensified white resistance.

Indeed, it appeared that in the aftermath of the *Brown* decision many white southerners dug in their heels in opposition to any and all black civil rights initiatives. In July 1954, just two months after *Brown*, the White Citizens' Council was formed in Sunflower County, Mississippi, to oppose racial integration. Within a few years, there would be a network of White Citizens' Councils across the nation, mainly in the South, with their membership reaching as high as 60,000. While much of the attention the White Citizens' Councils have received over the years has been focused on their racist rhetoric and propaganda, violence, and threats of violence, less well known are their highly coordinated efforts to use economic intimidation to thwart black progress. The Citizens' Councils used economic tactics against blacks who sought to register to vote, tried to enroll their children in white schools, or who were members of the NAACP. These tactics included calling in mortgages, denying loans and credit, and pressuring blacks who they controlled to boycott black-owned businesses. In some cities, councils published the names of African Americans who were members of the NAACP or who had signed petitions in favor of initiating school desegregation litigation. One Mississippi judge pointed out the economic consequences for blacks who sought to register to vote: "Over 95 per cent of the negroes [sic] of the South are employed by white men or corporations controlled by white men. A great many negro employees will be discharged and a deplorable situation will arise for the negro." Black professionals who catered to an exclusively black clientele were usually exempt from the economic pressures that the white community could exert on poorer blacks, but such was not always the case. After Dr. Clinton Battle tried to vote in Indianola, Mississippi, white plantation owners warned their sharecroppers not to go to the black physician. Deprived of patients, Battle was forced to abandon his practice and leave the state.[19]

The Louisiana Citizens' Council used the state law to disenfranchise blacks. Under Louisiana law, any two registered voters could challenge the qualifications of another voter. In thirteen parishes, Citizens' Council members pored over the books and had blacks purged from the rolls because of "errors" in their applications. In Ouachita Parish, 4,000 blacks had registered by September 1956, but as a result of various challenges, over 3,000 blacks lost their right to vote within the month.

Commonly referred to as the "daytime Klan," the White Citizens' Councils tried to portray their members as more respectable and sought to distance themselves from the white-sheeted Klansmen who operated mainly at night. But upon closer inspection of their motives and the violence their rhetoric inspired, one is hard-pressed to find any discernible difference. The Reverend George Lee, a grocery store owner and NAACP fieldworker in Belzoni, Mississippi, had been actively registering black voters since the early 1950s. In 1953 Lee and Gus Courts, another black grocer in the area, co-founded the Belzoni branch of the NAACP. Lee and Courts drew the attention of the Mississippi Citizens' Council when they complained to the Justice Department that local sheriff Ike Shelton refused to accept poll tax payments from blacks. To avoid a federal indictment, Shelton agreed to accept poll taxes without bias. As a result, Lee and Courts registered nearly all of the county's black voters in 1955. Angered by this show of black assertiveness, the local Citizens' Council began aggressively purging blacks from the voter rolls through intimidation and economic pressure. While many blacks caved under the pressure, neither Lee nor Courts backed down. Courts's landlord terminated his lease, forcing him to close his grocery store. The following month, on May 7, 1955, a car pulled alongside Lee's just before midnight, and an unidentified assailant fired three shotgun blasts into Lee's car, killing him instantly. No charges were ever brought.

A similar fate awaited Lamar Smith. A sixty-three-year-old farmer and World War I veteran, Smith had voted in the Mississippi primary election in August and had helped get others to the polls. A run-off election was scheduled for August 23. On August 13, 1955, while at the courthouse in Brookhaven, Mississippi, helping other blacks fill out absentee ballots, Smith was shot to death in broad daylight on the courthouse steps. Despite the presence of "dozens of" witnesses, including the local sheriff, no one was ever convicted of Smith's murder. Although three men were eventually arrested, an all-white jury refused to return any indictments against them.

Just fifteen days after Smith's murder, on August 28, fourteen-year-old Emmett Till from Chicago was murdered in Money, Mississippi, for allegedly flirting with a white woman. While visiting relatives in Mississippi, Till, along with some other boys, had gone into a local store to buy candy. Upon leaving the store, Till allegedly said "bye, baby" to Carolyn Bryant (some accounts claim he wolf whistled at her). Several days later Bryant's husband, Roy, along with his half-brother J. W. Milam, forcibly removed Till from the home of his great-uncle, Mose Wright. Bryant and Milam took Till to a barn where they proceeded to beat him savagely, gouging out one of his eyes before shooting him in the head and disposing of his body by dumping it in the Tallahatchie River, weighting it down with a 70-pound cotton gin fan tied around his neck with barbed wire. Three days later Till's bloated body was discovered and retrieved from the river. When the body was returned to Chicago (Mississippi authorities had initially insisted on a hasty local burial), Till's mother was determined to have a public funeral with an open casket so that the world might see, she said, "what they did to my son." Despite Bryant and Milam's admission that they had taken Till from the house, and the testimony of Mose Wright and another black man, Willie Reed, an all-white jury acquitted them. Protected against retrial by the defense of double jeopardy, Bryant and Milam later sold their story to journalist William Bradford Huie for $4,000, brazenly admitting how they had murdered the fourteen-year-old. They showed no remorse, nor did they believe they had done anything wrong.

When viewed within the broader context of the black freedom struggle, Emmett Till's senseless murder would serve as a haunting reminder that any black person, regardless of age, might pay the ultimate price for getting out of his or her "place," whether at a polling station or in a country store. Till's mutilated body on full display for the world to see served as a catalyst for a generation of black people who were determined to be treated as first-class citizens, regardless of the consequences. Till's murder, and the murders of the voting rights activists in particular, exposed the blatant racism of a federal government that refused to intervene to protect the constitutional rights of its black citizens and also underscored the hypocrisy of America's claim to be the leader of the free world. At a time when the Cold War was heating up, the Soviet Union never missed an opportunity to point out this moral inconsistency, especially to the nations of Asia and the newly independent black nations of Africa.

While it cannot be disputed that the *Brown* decision helped create a white backlash against African Americans' demands for racial equality, it is equally important to underscore that *Brown* energized black protest and raised it to a new level in the South and throughout the country. This critical fact is often minimized by those scholars who have promoted a "backlash thesis" which emphasizes the rise of Massive Resistance to the exclusion of the parallel escalation of black demands in light of *Plessy's* demise. *Brown* was a powerful symbol, and to generations of African Americans who had lived under the shadow of Jim Crow, it was a clarion call for protest, activism, and agency.[20]

Much of this agency occurred quietly behind the scenes with little notice or fanfare. For years, noted black educator and civil rights activist Septima Poinsette Clark had operated "citizenship schools" teaching literacy and citizenship rights. Often teaching in back rooms so as to elude the violence of racist whites, Mrs. Clark taught adults to read and to understand their rights as citizens, which in turn prompted many of them to seek empowerment through voting. In 1954 Mrs. Clark attended her first workshop at Highlander Folk School in Monteagle, Tennessee. Founded in 1932 by activist Myles Horton, Highlander became well known as an interracial social justice and leadership training school that played a critical role in the civil rights movement (many of the movement's future leaders, including Rosa Parks, Martin Luther King, Jr., and John Lewis, attended Highlander). Mrs. Clark's programs that focused on adult literacy as a prerequisite for voting were so successful that they were later emulated by other civil rights organizations, and as a result of her efforts in the face of increased white backlash, hundreds of thousands of African Americans became registered voters.

Despite ongoing (and sometimes successful) attempts by African Americans to obtain the right to vote in various local communities, events over the next ten years would overshadow those efforts as the civil rights movement began to unfold on the national stage.[21] On December 1, 1955, a forty-two-year-old black seamstress named Rosa Parks violated Montgomery, Alabama's, bus segregation ordinance by refusing to give her seat to a white passenger, thereby launching what became known as the Montgomery Bus Boycott. Twenty-six-year-old Martin Luther King, Jr., a native of Atlanta and the new pastor of Dexter Avenue Baptist Church, was elected president of the Montgomery Improvement Association and official spokesperson for the boycott. For the next thirteen months, African Americans in Montgomery refused to ride the city buses. While white city officials declined to make any modifications to the city's segregation ordinance, blacks took taxis, carpooled, and walked. The U.S. Supreme Court finally broke the impasse on November 13, 1956, in *Browder v. Gayle*, upholding a decision of a federal district court that segregation on Alabama's intrastate buses was unconstitutional.

The success of the Montgomery Bus Boycott had captured the nation's attention and had fired the imagination of African Americans across the country. At the same time, it had catapulted into prominence the young leader of the boycott, the Rev. Dr. Martin Luther King, Jr. A graduate of Morehouse College in Atlanta and Boston University, King had studied the writings of Henry David Thoreau as well as the successful pacifist movement Mohandas Gandhi had led in India against the powerful British Empire. In January 1957, the Southern Christian Leadership Conference (SCLC) was founded as a civil rights organization dedicated to direct, nonviolent social action to confront segregation. Dr. King was elected as the organization's first president. In September of that year, nine black students attempting to desegregate Central High School in Little Rock, Arkansas, were turned away by the Arkansas National Guard on orders by Governor Orval Faubus. President Dwight Eisenhower, who had never expressed support for the *Brown* decision, eventually sent in federal troops to enforce school desegregation. At the end of the 1957–58 school year, Faubus closed all of the high schools in the state to halt desegregation.

On February 1, 1960, four black students from North Carolina A&T University took seats at a "whites only" lunch counter at Woolworth's in Greensboro, North Carolina. This action was repeated twelve days later in Nashville, Tennessee. Soon, the "sit-ins" at segregated lunch counters had spread all across the South. In April, a group of young activists came together on the campus of Shaw University in Raleigh, North Carolina, and organized the Student Nonviolent Coordinating Committee (SNCC). The Congress of Racial Equality (CORE), founded in 1942, made its presence felt by launching the "freedom rides" challenging segregation on interstate buses in May 1961. The freedom riders were savagely beaten in Birmingham and Montgomery, one of the buses was firebombed outside of Anniston, Alabama, and many of the riders (which now included a contingent from SNCC since many of the riders from CORE had been too badly beaten to continue) were sentenced to lengthy jail terms in the notorious maximum security state penitentiary in Mississippi known as Parchman Farm.

The year 1963 would prove to be the most active yet on the civil rights front. After a disappointing campaign in Albany, Georgia, which lasted from the fall of 1961 to the spring of 1962 and failed to produce any tangible results, the SCLC confronted segregation in Birmingham, Alabama, in May, and the images of police dogs and firefighters' water hoses being used against black children would prove to be some of the most iconic of that era. On June 12, Mississippi's top NAACP activist, Medgar Evers, was shot to death in his driveway. For many years Evers had led voter registration campaigns state-wide, and his unyielding activism had made him a target of white supremacists for decades. Evers had been assassinated while other civil rights leaders were planning a major march on the nation's capital to highlight the need for strong civil rights legislation that had stalled in Congress. On August 28, 1963, nearly a quarter of a million people participated in the March on Washington, where Dr. Martin Luther King, Jr., delivered his "I Have a Dream" speech in the shadow of the Lincoln Memorial. Eighteen days later, dynamite planted by Klansmen at the 16th Street Baptist Church in Birmingham exploded, killing four young girls getting ready for Sunday school.

The violence that had accompanied the black freedom struggle reached the White House on November 22, 1963, when President John F. Kennedy was assassinated in Dallas, Texas. Many in the movement saw Kennedy's death as a tremendous loss for their cause, although there were those who had always believed that Kennedy's support for civil rights was political and tenuous at best. Civil rights leaders at first were unsure about Kennedy's vice president and successor Lyndon Baines Johnson of Texas. But just five days after Kennedy's assassination the new president addressed a joint session of Congress. "No memorial oration or eulogy could more eloquently honor President Kennedy's memory than the earliest possible passage of the civil rights bill for which he fought so long. We have talked long enough in this country about equal rights. We have talked for one hundred years or more. It is time now to write the next chapter, and to write it in the books of law."[22] The Civil Rights Act that Kennedy had submitted to Congress shortly before the March on Washington was the most comprehensive piece of legislation aimed at ending racial discrimination since Reconstruction. Even with Johnson's support, it was clear that the bill would face strong opposition in both houses of Congress, especially in the Senate, where southern segregationists controlled key committees. And while the bill had been crafted to outlaw racial segregation and discrimination in all publicly or privately owned facilities that catered to the general public, the legislation did little to address the one issue that civil rights leaders considered the most crucial—the right to vote.

Since the early 1960s various civil rights organizations had been working with blacks throughout the South helping them to understand the voting process as well as to overcome the fear many of them had come to associate with voting. Generations of African Americans had come of age in the South understanding all too well the consequences of trying to exercise their political power. Because of Mississippi's brutal history of racist violence and voter suppression, most of the efforts had been focused there. In 1962 several local civil rights groups in Mississippi had joined forces with the NAACP, CORE, SCLC, and SNCC to form the Council of Federated Organizations (COFO), which served as an umbrella group that sought to coordinate all of their voting activities. In an attempt to disprove segregationist claims that blacks were not interested in voting, COFO created the "Freedom Vote," which was merely a mock election in which unofficial "Freedom Party" candidates were placed on the ballots alongside Democratic and Republican candidates. The Freedom Vote proved to be very effective in raising black people's consciousness and political awareness, because as veteran SNCC activist Bob Moses put it, "eventually, black people were going to be electing people to office—black people to office."[23]

The Freedom Vote was so successful that COFO decided to launch an even more ambitious voting rights project the following summer. SNCC planned a major voter registration drive across the entire state of Mississippi and invited hundreds of students from across the nation to participate, including a good number of white students from the North. Some SNCC staffers opposed the idea of involving white students, believing that white outsiders would undermine the power of local blacks. But others felt differently, believing that the means of achieving black liberation had to be consistent with the end, and that anyone who wanted to participate, regardless of color, should be welcomed. Many in SNCC also understood that the presence of large numbers of whites in Mississippi would bring increased media coverage and possibly afford them some protection from racist violence. The project became known as "Freedom Summer."

On Saturday, June 20, 1964, the first wave of recruits left Oxford, Ohio, where they had undergone a week-long orientation, heading for Mississippi. Among them was Andrew Goodman, a twenty-year-old Queens College student from New York. On the next day Goodman, along with twenty-four-year-old Michael Schwerner, a veteran white activist in Mississippi whom Klansmen had nicknamed "Goatee," and twenty-one-year-old CORE worker James Chaney, a black Mississippi native, went to the town of Lawndale to investigate the burning of a black church. Sometime around 3:00 in the afternoon their blue Ford station wagon was stopped by Deputy Sheriff Cecil Price near the town of Philadelphia, Mississippi. The three were taken to jail, presumably on speeding charges, but were released later that night. Hours passed and no one at headquarters had heard from them (as a precaution, all civil rights workers were required to check in with Freedom Summer head-quarters at regular intervals). They all feared the worst.

The disappearance of the three civil rights workers was suddenly national news. President Johnson sent two hundred sailors to Mississippi to help in the search and also instructed FBI director J. Edgar Hoover to send agents to assist. Even as the search for Chaney, Goodman, and Schwerner continued to dominate the national news, racial violence in Mississippi went on unabated. A black church in the town of Clinton was burned after a white minister taught a Bible class there. Four whites shot at a car carrying Freedom Summer volunteers. Police in Columbus arrested seven workers for distributing infor-mation on voter registration. Meanwhile, the sailors and the agents searching for the missing men found the bodies of other blacks long missing, but these discoveries caused no public outcry. When these black bodies were found, re-calls CORE activist Dave Dennis, no one cared. "As soon as it was determined that they were not the three workers, then those deaths were forgotten."[24]

Within a week of the disappearances, President Johnson won a major vic-tory in the Senate. Johnson's political maneuvering had finally paid off as he was able to convince opponents of the controversial civil rights bill to end their filibuster. On July 2, 1964, President Johnson signed into law the Civil Rights Act of 1964, the most sweeping and comprehensive civil rights legisla-tion ever passed. Its purpose was to eliminate from American life the remain-ing vestiges of racial discrimination and segregation in all public facilities and accommodations. But the celebration was short-lived. One month later, on August 4, the bodies of the three civil rights workers were discovered. Acting on an anonymous tip from an informant known only as "Mr. X," who was reportedly paid $30,000, the FBI located the bodies in an earthen dam on a farm near Philadelphia, Mississippi. Goodman and Schwerner had each been shot once in the head; Chaney had been shot twice, and his skull had been fractured as the result of a savage beating. Mississippi segregationists, who had initially dismissed the disappearance of the three as a hoax aimed at generating public attention, were unrepentant. "When people leave any section of the country and go into another section looking for trouble," said Congressman Arthur Winstead, "they usually find it."[25] Eighteen white Mis-sissippians were eventually indicted on charges of conspiracy to commit mur-der. Although charges against the men were subsequently dropped in state court, six of the accused were later convicted for violating federal civil rights laws. Deputy Sheriff Cecil Price, a member of the White Knights of the Ku Klux Klan and the one who had stopped the three for speeding on June 21, served four and a half years of a six-year sentence—the longest term served by any of the convicted murderers.

Even as the Civil Rights Act of 1964 was heralded as an important milestone in the black freedom struggle, the murders of three civil rights workers highlighted not only the continuing racist terror in the Deep South but also the urgent need for stronger enforcement of existing civil rights laws. Civil rights workers in Mississippi and elsewhere were painfully aware that many of the hardships they endured daily came from elected officials who governed every aspect of their lives, from the police force to the governor's mansion. The need for African Americans to take control of their lives by having the freedom to vote had been powerfully dramatized with Freedom Summer, and the murders of the three civil rights workers was the ultimate price to be paid for that freedom. As important as the Civil Rights Act of 1964 was, it had not addressed the issue of voting. Although voting rights had been included as part of the bill, segregationist lawmakers and their allies had used their influence to weaken that provision before the bill was sent to the floor for a final vote. But events in Mississippi in 1964, beginning with Freedom Summer and culminating in the formation of the Mississippi Freedom Democratic Party, had once again focused the nation's attention on the need for stronger voting rights legislation. The next chapter in the civil rights movement would be written in Selma, Alabama.

2

Seeds of Protest

We had decided that we were going to get killed or we [were] going to be free.
                                        —Albert Turner, Selma, Alabama, 1965

AT THE BEGINNING OF 1963, after years of litigation and intensive efforts by SNCC to increase black voter registration and participation, only 353 of the approximately 15,000 African Americans who were of voting age—a mere 2.1 percent—were enrolled in Dallas County, Alabama, within which Selma was located. By contrast, roughly 65 percent of eligible whites were registered. Blacks made up approximately half of the voting-age population in Dallas County but held none of the elective positions. At that time SNCC had only two workers in Selma, and with most of the civil rights activity having centered around Montgomery or Birmingham, there was little to indicate that Selma was about to become the focal point for a major civil rights campaign.

All of that, however, was about to change with the arrival of Bernard Lafayette. As a young seminary student in Nashville, Tennessee, in 1960 when the sit-ins began, Lafayette became involved with the fledgling Student Nonviolent Coordinating Committee. The very next year, 1961, he participated in the Freedom Rides. He had expressed an early interest in voter registration work, but before he received an assignment to direct his own field project he was dispatched to Detroit and Chicago to help raise money for activists who had been jailed in Louisiana for engaging in voter registration. By the time he returned to Atlanta, all of the field assignments had been made. Seeing the disappointment in Lafayette's face, SNCC executive secretary James Forman then presented him with several options. He could join SNCC's Arkansas project and work with its director Bill Hanson, work with Charles Sherrod in Southwest Georgia, or work with Bob Moses in Mississippi. The expression on Lafayette's face, however, revealed that he found none of these options satisfactory.

A committed activist who had been badly beaten during the freedom rides, Lafayette believed that he had earned an assignment as a project director, not as someone else's assistant. As Lafayette continued to press the point, Forman paused for a moment and then considered one last option. There was one place where Lafayette could direct his own project, but SNCC had initially crossed it off their list, saying that the potential for bloodshed was too great. That place was Selma, Alabama. Veteran Selma activist Amelia Boynton, who had been a registered voter since 1932, had been trying for years to get the national civil rights organizations to come to Selma. Forman had considered it, but had been reluctant. He had a United States map tacked to the wall with all the southern states highlighted, and there was a big red X marked through the entire state of Alabama. Two previous groups of SNCC volunteers had tried to organize in Alabama, but both groups came back with the same report: "whites were too mean, and blacks were too afraid." Forman turned to Lafayette and said, "Well, you can go to Selma to check it out if you want." Lafayette's face immediately lit up. "I don't want to check it out," he replied. "I'll take it." Once he began doing research on Selma, however, he quickly comprehended why SNCC had crossed it off the list, and he realized that Forman had not exaggerated the danger. But Lafayette was undeterred, and in the fall of 1962 he headed to Montgomery for a series of meetings with veteran activists who would give him some idea of what he was in for.[1]

In February 1963 Bernard and Colia Lafayette came to Selma to begin a voter education effort. Throughout the spring their monthly voting clinics, in which they taught would-be voters how to properly fill out the required forms, drew an average of forty people. Complicating the Lafayettes' efforts was the notion, prevalent among blacks, that voting was "white folks' business." Several African American ministers, fearing retribution from local whites, were reluctant to host voter registration meetings in their churches. This renewed interest in voting had been eyed suspiciously by local whites for several weeks, and their attention was piqued further in mid-June when more than seven hundred blacks turned out to a mass rally at which SCLC's James Bevel spoke. Now the local chapter of the Citizens' Council was taking notice, as was Dallas County's sheriff, James G. Clark, Jr.

The Lafayettes and other SNCC activists were now being subjected to a series of arrests and intimidation. At even the smallest gathering, police showed up to harass people. Sheriff Clark had begun sending officers to meetings to record the names of those present; those in attendance would then be threatened with economic retaliation. On June 26 the Justice Department filed a request for a restraining order against Sheriff Clark, but a local judge denied the request the same day, and his ruling was upheld by the appeals court the following day. Given this atmosphere of heightened tension and fear, it is not surprising that turnout at the voting clinics declined dramatically, especially as it now appeared evident that Sheriff Jim Clark's word was law.

In September 1963 SNCC activist Worth Long arrived in Selma, and he and some others initiated a lunch counter sit-in. Their sit-in resulted in several arrests, which prompted a protest march, which led to additional arrests. Later that month SNCC president John Lewis and SNCC executive secretary James Forman arrived and decided to turn the focus of the campaign back to voting rights. African Americans in Selma who were courageous enough to go to the courthouse in an attempt to register soon discovered that being able to do so was virtually impossible. The registration office was open only on the first and third Mondays of each month, and registrars usually arrived late, took long lunch breaks, and left early. And getting into the registrar's office was no guarantee of getting registered, as literacy tests still effectively disqualified the vast majority of black applicants.

On October 7, 1963, SNCC organized a Freedom Day voter registration drive in which nearly three hundred black would-be voters lined up at the Dallas County courthouse. With four FBI agents and two Justice Department attorneys looking on, Sheriff Clark and his deputies harassed the applicants and prevented SNCC workers from bringing them food and water while they waited in line. Clark had a local photographer take pictures of every person in line and asked the people how their employers might react to seeing their pictures. Despite Clark's efforts to keep the national press from getting too close to the action, the story and photos did reach Washington. The civil rights legislation that was then pending in Congress was aimed at ending discrimination in public accommodations, but it did not address the issue of voting rights. Throughout 1963 and into 1964 the NAACP's chief Washington lobbyist Clarence Mitchell worked hard to have voting rights protections incorporated into the pending civil rights bill, but his efforts were in vain.[2]

On July 2, 1964, President Johnson signed the Civil Rights Act into law, and almost immediately Clarence Mitchell and other civil rights leaders began pressuring the president for additional legislation to guarantee voting rights. While not necessarily opposed to such legislation, Johnson did not see it as a priority. He was reluctant to move too soon on any additional civil rights legislation on the heels of the recently passed bill. Still, he asked Attorney General Nicholas Katzenbach to prepare a strategy memo on when and how a voting rights bill might be drafted.

Such legislation was badly needed in places like Selma, where blacks attempting to register were often better educated than the registrars who challenged them. Selma resident and school teacher Amelia Boynton witnessed one occasion when a white official had trouble reading the questions to a black teacher. Seeing that the registrar was having difficulty pronouncing the words, the black teacher finally said, "Those words are 'constitutionality' and 'interrogatory.'" The registrar turned red with anger, Mrs. Boynton recalled, and not surprisingly, the teacher failed the test. As one of Selma's few registered black voters, Mrs. Boynton was occasionally called upon to vouch for the character of other blacks trying to register, in accordance with Alabama law. One day an elderly black man with an unsteady hand asked Mrs. Boynton to help him write his address as he stood before the registrar. "I can't write so good," he explained. The registrar then told him to get out of line if he couldn't write his own address. "Mr. Adkins," the black man told the registrar, "I am 65 years old, I own 100 acres of land that is paid for, I am a taxpayer and I have six children. All of them is teachin', workin' . . . If what I done ain't enough to be a registered voter with all the tax I got to pay, then Lord have mercy on America."[3]

Despite mounting local white opposition and resistance, SNCC activists continued to press on, working with the Dallas County Voters League, an organization founded in the 1930s. They explained to local blacks that the right to vote was about much more than choosing who they wanted to represent them in government, but that the larger issues were political leverage and holding their elected officials accountable. Political power meant that

Selma's black residents could get their streets paved, ensure that their trash was picked up, and force the school board to allocate more money to black schools, which in Selma were still totally segregated and grossly underfunded. If local blacks were willing to challenge the system by registering, they could destroy the system of "whites only" political domination. And if local whites tried to block their efforts, SNCC activists assured them that the federal government would step in to protect them. "Our strategy," James Forman wrote later, "was to force the U.S. government to intervene in case there were arrests—and if they did not intervene, that inaction would once again prove the government was not on our side and thus intensify the development of a mass consciousness among blacks."[4]

While passage of the Civil Rights Act brought about few, if any, changes to the racial situation in Selma, the bill did prompt a revival of protest activity. Blacks felt that even if they could not vote, they could test the limits of this new civil rights legislation. On July 4 several blacks attempted to attend an all-white theater and were attacked by whites, and four blacks who attempted to desegregate a restaurant were arrested on trespassing charges. On July 5 SNCC held a voter registration rally, after which Sheriff Jim Clark's deputies used nightsticks and tear gas on the demonstrators. Newsmen and photographers were also attacked by Clark's deputies and were later ordered out of town. On July 6 John Lewis led about fifty blacks to the courthouse in an attempt to register; once there they were beaten by Clark's deputies before being arrested. A few days later state circuit judge James Hare issued an injunction forbidding public gatherings of more than three people. While the Justice Department prepared complaints against local judicial authorities, voting rights protest ground to a halt in the latter half of 1964.[5]

Dr. Martin Luther King's "I Have a Dream" speech, delivered at the March on Washington on August 28, 1963, perhaps for the first time positioned the black freedom struggle on the world stage, and King was front and center of it. King's philosophy of nonviolent social protest had become the overarching theme of the movement, and his efforts "to redeem the soul of America"— SCLC's slogan—drew obvious comparisons to Gandhi's protest movement in India. In December 1964 King traveled to Norway to accept the Nobel Peace Prize, calling himself a "trustee for the twenty-two million Negroes of the United States of America who are engaged in a creative battle to end the night of racial injustice."[6] Since early November, King and his SCLC staffers had been planning for a voting rights demonstration in Alabama, but they were not entirely sure where specifically they should concentrate their efforts. A meeting with President Johnson, however, would soon provide King with the clarity he needed.

On his way back from Oslo, Norway, after having accepting the Nobel Peace Prize, King and a few of his staffers went to Washington, D.C., to meet with President Johnson. King had been pressing the president for voting rights legislation for some time, but Johnson remained noncommittal. Believing that he had already spent all of his political capital in securing the passage of the 1964 Civil Rights Act, Johnson devoted an hour or more trying to convince King why he could not introduce any new civil rights legislation to Congress. As Andrew Young remembers, Johnson told King, "I just can't do that right now. There will be filibusters, and all kinds of resistance. You know that. I just don't have the power." Young, clearly dejected upon leaving the White House, turned to King and asked him, "Well, what do you think about that?" With a look half serious and half playful, King turned to Young and said, "I'll just have to figure out a way to get the president some power." In that moment, King made the decision to go to Selma.[7]

King's plan to launch a voting rights campaign in Selma was unwelcomed news to Selma's white political establishment, especially Selma's new mayor Joseph Smitherman. Elected in the fall of 1964, Smitherman had campaigned on a promise to bring industry to Selma. Although a committed segregationist, he was shrewder politically than his predecessor and had sense enough to know that violent bloody confrontations with civil rights protestors were not good for business. With images of Bull Connor's brutality against black schoolchildren in Birmingham the previous year still fresh in the nation's collective memory, Smitherman was not eager for a repeat performance in Selma. To keep a lid on the situation, Smitherman relied on Wilson Baker, Selma's new public safety director. A former Selma police captain, Baker had lost out to Jim Clark in his bid to become sheriff of Dallas County. After the election, Smitherman appointed Baker to the newly created position of public safety director. Baker's role was to enforce the law within the city of Selma, while Clark would handle law enforcement within the county. But the way he saw it—and undoubtedly, the way it was perceived by others—Jim Clark was still the highest ranking law enforcement officer in Selma.

Upon learning of King's plan to bring his organization to Selma, Mayor Smitherman sent Baker to see Burke Marshall, assistant attorney general and head of the Civil Rights Division at the Justice Department, in an attempt to get Marshall to convince King not to come. Baker said that he wanted to avoid bloodshed in Selma, and that he would do his utmost to prevent violence, but that King's presence would inflame an already volatile situation. Baker emphasized that it was not he but rather Sheriff Clark who would be more prone to violence, and he warned that he could not promise that he would be able to contain Clark if King came to town. Marshall called King to convey Baker's concerns, but King's response was brief. Hanging up the phone, Marshall turned to Baker and said, "They're coming to Selma . . . They've already put too much work on the project to turn back now."[8]

King arrived in Selma on January 2, 1965, and later that evening spoke to a congregation of about seven hundred at Brown Chapel African Methodist Episcopal Church. King told those in attendance that there would be massive demonstrations if Dallas County did not begin to register its black citizens in large numbers. If appeals to Alabama governor George C. Wallace and to the state legislature went unheeded, King said, "We will seek to arouse the federal government by marching by the thousands." And if that did not work, King promised another march on Washington "to appeal to the conscience of the Congress." King said that Selma had been chosen for this voting rights campaign because "it has become a symbol of bitter-end resistance to the civil rights movement in the Deep South."[9]

In an attempt to keep the lid on a potentially explosive situation, Baker had asked Sheriff Clark to avoid any kind of police brutality that would gain national headlines. Both Baker and Mayor Smitherman knew that King was fully aware of Clark's reputation for violence against blacks and believed that King had selected Selma for precisely that reason. For his part, Clark saw no need to change his behavior, no matter how many reporters and cameras were in Selma. Some local white moderates had tried to convince the county registration board to ease their voter registration requirements temporarily while Selma was in the national spotlight, but their pleas fell on deaf ears. In fact, state circuit court judge James Hare, an avowed opponent of voting rights for blacks and a dependable Clark ally who had prevented more than three blacks from gathering together in one place, and Clark himself only made the situation worse in a series of statements given to the press. When national reporters asked why there were so few blacks registered to vote, Sheriff Clark said that it was "largely because of their mental I.Q." Judge Hare told another reporter, "You see, most of your Selma Negroes are descended from the Ebo [sic] and Angola tribes of Africa. You could never teach or trust an Ebo back in slave days, and even today I can spot their tribal characteristics. They have protruding heels, for instance."[10]

On Thursday evening, January 14, King told a crowd of eight hundred that they would soon begin testing the public accommodations provisions of the 1964 Civil Rights Act, which would be coordinated with a gathering at the courthouse for the purpose of voter registration. The next day, the Justice Department filed suit in Montgomery against Alabama's statewide registration test, charging that its difficult standards violated Title I of the 1964 act. By Sunday, the 17th, King's aides were saying that Selma city officials had assured them no arrests would be made on Monday at the courthouse and that protection would be given to peaceful attempts to register. Sheriff Clark, they said, had been told not to interfere.

On Monday morning, January 18, SCLC successfully "tested" seven Selma restaurants without incident, after which King and SNCC's John Lewis led some four hundred blacks in the campaign's first march to the courthouse, defying the court order against congregating. Baker was aware that King and SCLC wanted to create another Birmingham-like situation in Selma, but he steered clear of any confrontation and refused to make any arrests. When Sheriff Clark arrived, those who had been standing in line were herded into an alley behind the courthouse; there was no violence, but no one was allowed to register. King understood that unless there was violence, journalists from the national press would lose interest and the campaign might fizzle out. SCLC planned to march again the following day.

When the demonstrators gathered at the courthouse on Tuesday morning, January 19, they refused to obey Clark's orders to wait in the alley. Clark then ordered the group off of the courthouse sidewalk, and when local activist Amelia Boynton was slow to move, Clark grabbed her by the back of her collar and, using his nightstick, violently shoved her for half a block into a patrol car. Observing the incident from a car across the street, King went inside the federal building, located directly across from the courthouse, and asked a Justice Department representative to take court action against Clark, whose action King later described as "one of the most brutal and unlawful acts I have seen an officer commit."[11] The following day the incident made the national news, being reported in the *New York Times* and the *Washington Post*.

On the same day that Mrs. Boynton was arrested, Clark's deputies detained sixty-seven other marchers. While SCLC staffers were pleased that Clark seemed to be losing his composure, Baker and Mayor Smitherman were describing Clark as "out of control,"[12] something that obviously jeopardized their strategy of keeping Selma away from the national limelight. With speaking engagements elsewhere, King had to leave Selma for a while, but the movement did not falter in his absence, and plans were made to intensify the protest.

On Wednesday, January 20, three groups of marchers confronted Sheriff Clark at the courthouse. Clark arrested the first two groups for blocking the sidewalk and for unlawful assembly. When the third group arrived, Public Safety Director Baker told them that they could use the front entrance (which Clark had refused them) so long as they did not obstruct the sidewalk. But Clark blocked that move, and for the next several minutes, with Baker and Clark glaring at each other, the tension between the two men was palpable. Clark finally announced to the marchers that they had one minute to move, and when they did not, he ordered his deputies to arrest them.

On Friday, January 22, with King back in Selma, more than one hundred black school teachers descended upon the courthouse to voice their displeasure with both the voting registration procedures as well as Sheriff Clark's rough treatment of their colleague Amelia Boynton. They were led by Rev. Frederick Reese, who served as president of both the Dallas County Voters League and the Selma Teachers Association. School teachers had traditionally enjoyed an elite status within the African American community but had generally steered clear of civil rights protest activity for fear of being fired by the white school board.

The teachers began to march up the courthouse steps and were met at the top by the school board chairman and the superintendent of schools, who tried to persuade them to leave. When they did not, Sheriff Clark and five deputies emerged from the courthouse with their nightsticks in hand. "This courthouse is a serious place of business," Clark said, "and you seem to think you can take it just to be Disneyland or something on parade. Do you have business in this courthouse?" Rev. Frederick Reese then replied, "The only business we have is to come to the Board of Registrars to register." Sheriff Clark replied, "The Board of Registrars is not in session . . . You came down here to make a mockery out of this courthouse and we're not going to have it." When the teachers refused to move, Clark poked them with his nightstick, forcing them down the steps. Rev. Reese later explained, "So I saw then that he was not going to arrest us, as I really wanted him to do. Therefore, we asked the teachers then to regroup and we marched back, not to the school but to Brown Chapel Church, at which time there was a rally held."[13]

The teachers' protest march to the courthouse provided a welcomed spark to the movement, and SCLC's Andrew Young later described it as "the most significant thing that has happened in the racial movement since Birmingham." Rachel West Nelson and Sheyann Webb, both schoolchildren at the time, later remembered how significant the teachers' march was. "People looked up to teachers then, they looked up to preachers. They were somewhat leaders for us back then," said Nelson. Webb recalls how the teachers' mobilization led directly to more children getting involved. "It was amazing to see how many teachers had participated. I remember vividly on that day when I saw my teachers marching with me . . . just for the right to vote." Once the teachers got involved, the rest of Selma's black citizens began to mobilize. As Rev. Reese recalls, "Then the undertakers got a group and they marched. The beauticians got a group, they marched. Everybody marched after the teachers marched because teachers had more influence than they ever dreamed in the community."[14]

On Sunday, January 24, King departed Selma for Atlanta and no marches were held, but they resumed in full force on Monday, the 25th. In one of the campaign's most memorable marches, fifty-three-year-old Annie Lee Cooper chose to resist Sheriff Clark's tactics. When Mrs. Cooper stepped out of the line of marchers, Clark jabbed her with his elbow and ordered her to get back in line, but what happened next surprised all of the onlookers. Rather than obey Clark's order, Mrs. Cooper turned and delivered a powerful blow to Clark's head, sending him reeling. As Clark began to fall, she hit him again. Two deputies tried to wrestle her to the ground, but she broke loose, ran back to Clark, and hit him again. Finally, three deputies managed to subdue her while Clark struck her in the head with his nightstick. She was later taken off to jail in two pairs of handcuffs with a wound over her right eye. The next day, photographs of Clark raising his stick over Mrs. Cooper's head as deputies held her down appeared on page 1 of the *New York Times* and page 2 of the *Washington Post*. The negative press was something that Mayor Smitherman and Public Safety Director Baker had hoped to avoid, but it was a victory for the movement.[15]

King returned to Selma on Sunday, January 31, and on that following Monday morning he addressed a crowd of more than 250 that he was preparing to lead downtown to the courthouse. "If Negroes could vote," King told the crowd, "there would be no Jim Clarks, there would be no oppressive poverty directed against Negroes, our children would not be crippled by segregated schools . . ."[16] King then led the marchers in a continuous line, deliberately ignoring the city ordinance that they break into smaller groups, as they had done previously. On this day, King was inviting arrest. The marchers had only gone a short distance when Director Baker halted the column and threatened to arrest the marchers if they did not break up into smaller groups. When they continued to march in an uninterrupted line, Baker placed the demonstrators, including King, under arrest. The local residents were released without bail, but King and his chief lieutenant Rev. Ralph D. Abernathy were offered bail but chose to remain in jail.

Once they learned of King's arrest, more than five hundred of Selma's black schoolchildren marched to the courthouse and were promptly arrested. Wednesday brought the arrests of more than four hundred additional marchers, including another three hundred schoolchildren. Selma's jails were now being filled to capacity, and the evening news was covering the mass arrests. Stories of brutality inside the jails, unsanitary conditions (there were no toilets, only buckets), and general mistreatment of the prisoners began to circulate widely, with some comparing the conditions to those of a prison camp. The situation in Selma had finally gotten the attention of some in Congress; Senator Jacob Javits, a New York Republican, called the mass arrests "shocking" because the marchers were seeking "the most basic right guaranteed by the Constitution." Javits then contacted the Justice Department, saying that Selma should "be watched closely to see whether additional law is now necessary."[17] Meanwhile, King sent telegrams to several congressmen expressing his concern that current laws did not adequately protect the rights of blacks seeking to vote.

A bipartisan congressional delegation consisting of fifteen northern members of the House of Representatives traveled to Selma to assess the situation. Congressman Charles Diggs, a black Democrat from Michigan, said that "I think it's a general consensus of the delegation—which was bipartisan . . . [and] made up of Negro and white congressmen from various parts of the county—that new legislation is going to be necessary if Negroes are going to be able to exercise the franchise as freely in the South . . . as they can in Detroit, New York, California, and places like that."[18] Meanwhile, SCLC's Andrew Young called the White House to ask that an emissary be sent to Selma to monitor the situation and to report back to the president. He also asked that President Johnson make a statement in support of voting rights and to prepare legislation to guarantee those rights.

On February 4, SCLC staffers were surprised to learn that Malcolm X, who had just spoken at a rally at Tuskegee Institute, was on his way to Selma and that he wanted permission to speak at the mass meeting that afternoon. Unbeknownst to SCLC, members of SNCC had invited Malcolm X to Selma to energize the campaign (or, as some in SCLC surmised, to undermine King, who was still in jail). During his years as national spokesman for the Nation of Islam, Malcolm X had eschewed involvement in politics and the civil rights movement, presumably because Nation of Islam founder Elijah Muhammad disapproved of both. Further, Malcolm's militant rhetoric ran counter to King's message of nonviolence, and he rarely disguised his disdain for what he termed "those Uncle Tom Negro leaders." But after his break with Elijah Muhammad in early 1964, Malcolm X had tried to reinvent himself as some-one who belonged on the civil rights movement's national stage alongside King; and SNCC activists, some of whom were moving closer to Malcolm's militant philosophy, were happy to accommodate.[19] But given Malcolm's past inflammatory rhetoric, some in SCLC were understandably reluctant to give him a public forum in Selma, fearing that his speech might erode support for their nonviolent movement. SCLC's Bernard Lafayette, one of the original organizers of the Selma campaign, argued in favor of allowing Malcolm to speak, saying that people should not be judged by their past actions, but on their intentions. After much debate, it was agreed that Malcolm would be permitted to speak.

Whatever SCLC's initial concerns or SNCC's intentions, Malcolm X's pres-ence in Selma proved to be supportive rather than disruptive, and it gave him an opportunity, albeit brief, to insert himself into a nonviolent movement. He had already reassured Coretta Scott King that he had not come to Selma to cause any difficulty for her husband, but to show support. Once he stepped up to the podium, this tall and imposing figure with the reddish-brown hair and trademark black frame glasses was unmistakably Malcolm X. Directing his words to the white media, Malcolm told the overflow crowd at Brown Chapel that "You had better listen to Dr. Martin Luther King, Jr., or you will have to listen to me. Dr. King wants the same thing I want—Freedom!" Malcolm ended his speech with "I'm not intending to try and stir you up and make you do something that you wouldn't have done anyway," at which the crowd burst into laughter and applause. He concluded, "I pray that God will bless you in everything that you do . . . And I pray that all the fear that has ever been in your heart will be taken out." Malcolm X's appearance in Selma was more significant than anyone could have known at the time. Seventeen days later, on February 21, he was assassinated as he prepared to lecture at the Audubon Ballroom in Harlem.[20]

On the same day as Malcolm X's speech in Selma, President Johnson held a press conference in Washington, D.C., to express his support of voting rights, his first direct response to the Selma campaign. "I should like to say that all Americans should be indignant when one American is denied the right to vote. The loss of that right to a single citizen undermines the freedom of every citizen. This is why all of us should be concerned with the efforts of our fellow Americans to register to vote in Alabama. . . . Nothing is more fundamental to American citizenship and to our freedom as a nation and as a people. I intend to see that that right is secured for all our citizens."[21]

On Friday morning, February 5, as the congressional delegation headed for Selma in response to SCLC's letter and telegrams, a letter from King appeared on page 15 of the *New York Times*. Entitled "A Letter from a Selma, Alabama, Jail," King's letter expressed a sentiment similar to that of his 1963 "Letter from Birmingham Jail" in which he condemned Birmingham's white moderates for their acquiescence to segregation and discrimination. King wrote:

> When the King of Norway participated in awarding the Nobel Peace Prize to me, he surely did not think that in less than sixty days I would be in jail. He, and almost all world opinion, will be shocked because they are little aware of the unfinished business in the South. . . . When the Civil Rights Act of 1964 was passed, many decent Americans were lulled into complacency because they thought the days of difficult struggle were over. Why are we in jail? Have you ever been required to answer 100 questions on government, some abstruse even to a political scientist, merely to vote? Have you ever stood in line with over a hundred others and after waiting an entire day seen less than ten given the qualifying test? This is Selma, Alabama, where there are more Negroes in jail with me than there are on the voting rolls."[22]

At the White House on the following day, presidential press secretary George Reedy announced that President Johnson would make "a strong recommendation" to Congress on voting rights legislation at some point in the future, but he offered no other specifics. King traveled to Washington hoping for a meeting with the president, but was told that Johnson was preoccupied with Vietnam, but that there was the possibility that the two men might be able to meet very soon. Back in Selma, no protests were held on that Saturday or Sunday as SCLC prepared for Monday, February 8, the next day that the registration board would be in session.

On that Monday morning, SCLC staffer James Bevel and a group of about fifty went to the courthouse mainly to protest a new voter registration procedure that Selma city officials had devised. Under this new policy, blacks wishing to register could sign a ledger, or an "appearance book," and would be served first on the two days per month when the registrar's office was open. SCLC viewed this as a stalling tactic, something that would give the false impression that Selma officials were making some concessions to blacks when in fact they were merely maintaining the status quo. Bevel and his group wanted to complete the entire registration process on the spot, without having to wait, and thus made their intentions known to the registrar. Upon being refused, they walked out of the office only to be confronted by Sheriff Clark who, according to reporters, was "shaking with anger." Clark began jabbing Bevel in the abdomen with his nightstick and then grabbed his shoulders and forced him backwards down the courthouse steps. "I have a constitutional right," Bevel began, at which time Clark shouted, "You get out of here," and then continued to use his nightstick to push Bevel down the steps. Clark and two of his deputies then arrested the entire group.[23]

There were two important developments on the following day, February 9. Nineteen members of the House of Representatives delivered comments on the floor in support of stronger voting rights legislation. Charles Diggs of Michigan and William Ryan of New York, both of whom were part of the congressional delegation to Selma, read from depositions they had received from some of Selma's black residents that painted a chilling portrait of the experience of African Americans in Selma who tried to register. Other congressmen took the floor to condemn the conduct of the law enforcement personnel in Selma and Dallas County. On the same day, King finally got his meeting with President Johnson. King met with Vice President Hubert Humphrey and Attorney General Nicholas Katzenbach for about ninety minutes, and then with the president for about fifteen minutes. After the meetings King appeared hopeful, reporting to the press that "The president made it very clear to me

For years, African Americans in Selma had tried in vain to register to vote. The registrar's office was located inside the Dallas County Courthouse, and gaining access was almost impossible for Selma's black residents. Here, Sheriff Jim Clark points a billy club and an electric prod at blacks to prevent them from entering the courthouse. Blacks who did not leave when ordered to do so were subject to arrest or a physical assault from either Sheriff Clark or his deputies. Prints and Photographs Division, Library of Congress

that he was determined during his administration to see all remaining obstacles removed to the right of Negroes to vote."[24]

Congressional condemnation of Selma's law enforcement tactics had apparently not fazed Sheriff Clark, who on Wednesday, February 10, arrested 165 marching teenagers and sent them on a "forced march" out into the countryside. Although news reporters were not allowed to follow, the children later reported that Clark's deputies had used nightsticks and cattle prods to keep them running at a quickened pace. News of this angered Selma's black community and resulted in large turnouts at that evening's two rallies, and press reports the following day stated that Clark's actions had revived the campaign. Adding additional fuel to the fire were reports that James Bevel, who had been transferred from the jail to an infirmary when he developed a fever, had been chained to his bed with leg-irons despite doctors' protests.[25]

On Friday, February 12, Sheriff Clark entered the hospital himself, suffering from exhaustion. He remained there until the following Monday. During his brief convalescence, focus shifted to Washington, where Attorney General Katzenbach had a series of meetings with lawmakers who were continuing to press him on the specifics of just what legislative ideas the president had in mind. But Katzenbach remained vague, simply telling the congressmen to forward their suggestions to the Justice Department. Robert F. Kennedy, former attorney general and recently elected U.S. senator from New York, shared his belief that there would not be any significant progress in voting rights as long as literacy tests were being used throughout the South. Kennedy believed that those could only be eliminated by constitutional amendment, and he reportedly concluded, "It will take many a year for Negro voting rights to be a reality in the South."[26]

On Tuesday, February 16, SCLC's Reverend C. T. Vivian led roughly twenty-five marchers to the courthouse in the rain to protest the city's new voter registration policy. As he had done a few days earlier with James Bevel, Sheriff Clark appeared at the top of the courthouse steps to refuse admittance to Vivian and his group, at which time Vivian began to lecture Clark and his deputies:

> And we want you to know, gentlemen, that every one of you, we know your badge numbers, we know your names. There were those that followed Hitler, like you blindly follow this Sheriff Clark who didn't think their day was coming. But they also were pulled into courtrooms and they were also given their death sentences. You're not this bad a racist, but you're a racist in the same way Hitler was a racist. And you're blindly following a man that's leading you down a road that's going to bring you into federal court. . . . For this is not a local problem, gentlemen. This is a national problem. You can't keep anyone in the United States from voting without hurting the rights of all other citizens. Democracy is built on this. This is why every man has the right to vote, regardless. . . . And this is what we're trying to say to you. These people have the right to stand inside this courthouse. If you'd had your basic civics course, you'd know this, gentlemen.[27]

Despite the best efforts of his deputies to restrain him, Clark lost his temper. Angered by Vivian's lecture on American democracy and the light bulbs of television cameramen shining in his face, Clark suddenly lunged at Vivian, hitting him in the mouth with a blow that sent him reeling. Dazed and bleeding, Vivian continued, "If we're wrong, why don't you arrest us? You don't have to beat us. . . . We're willing to be beaten for democracy, and you misuse democracy in the street. You beat people bloody in order that they will not have the privilege to vote."[28]

The courthouse confrontation between Sheriff Clark and Reverend Vivian, and the physical assault that followed, provided powerful footage on the evening news. In an attempt to deny their own culpability, Mayor Smitherman and Wilson Baker told reporters that Jim Clark alone was responsible for the violence. But at a mass meeting the following evening, Martin Luther King saw it quite differently. Speaking to an overflow crowd at Brown Chapel, King said: "I'm here to tell you tonight that the businessmen, the mayor of this city, the police commissioner of this city, and everybody in the white power structure of this city must take a responsibility for everything that Jim Clark does. It's time for us to say to these men that if you don't do something about it, we will have no alternative but to engage in broader and more drastic forms of civil disobedience in order to bring the attention of a nation to this whole issue in Selma, Alabama."[29]

King's call for "broader and more drastic forms of civil disobedience" meant that now there would be nighttime marches, and that the voting rights campaign, which had up to this point been confined to Selma, would now extend to other nearby towns. One of those towns was Marion, where SCLC staffer Rev. James Orange had been leading the voter registration effort. Standing more than 6'3" tall and weighing over 300 pounds, Orange was physically imposing but deeply committed to nonviolence. Referred to by many as the "gentle giant," Orange endured numerous beatings and more than a hundred arrests over the years as a result of his civil rights activism, but his dedication to both the movement and nonviolence never wavered.

While leading the effort in Marion, Orange had marched along with roughly six hundred students to the courthouse and they were all subsequently arrested. But after the students were released, Orange was detained on additional charges of contributing to the delinquency of minors because his voter registration campaign had involved students. While Orange was still incarcerated, a deputy approached him with a rope that had a noose tied at the end of it and then hung it from the top of his jail cell. A black inmate who had just been released from the same jail (apparently for public drunkenness)

Rev. C. T. Vivian of the Southern Christian Leadership Conference leading prayer on the steps of the Dallas County Courthouse, while Sheriff Clark looks at his watch and tells Vivian "time's up." Following his prayer, Reverend Vivian lectured Sheriff Clark and his deputies on the evils of racism. Moments later, Clark physically assaulted Vivian, hitting him with such force that Clark fractured a finger on his left hand. Reverend Vivian and the marchers accompanying him were later arrested and charged with unlawful assembly. Prints and Photographs Division, Library of Congress

claimed to have overheard a plot by a group of Klansmen to lynch Orange while he was in custody. Word of the plot against Reverend Orange's life soon reached the students, who quickly ran to the church where a rally was being held. SCLC then hastily planned a protest march for the purpose of calling attention to Orange's illegal incarceration, as well as to provide him with some measure of protection, hoping that the presence of dozens of marchers would deter any Klan activity. Meanwhile back in Selma, Reverend C. T. Vivian received a desperate call to come to Marion to speak at the evening's rally.

On the evening of February 18, Reverend Vivian gave a fiery speech at a mass meeting at Zion United Methodist Church in Marion before leading a large group of marchers out of the church down the sidewalk toward the nearby courthouse. After having gone no further than a block, what was described as a "sizeable detachment" of state troopers appeared, headed by Col. Al Lingo. Also on the scene were auxiliary police and a large gathering of angry white civilians. The marchers were ordered to turn around and return to their church. Suddenly, without warning, the streetlights went out (it was later confirmed that they had been turned off by the power company), and the state troopers began to attack the marchers with their nightsticks. As the marchers stumbled over each other in an attempt to seek cover or to return to the church, the white onlookers joined in the melee, attacking both the marchers and the press contingent that had been standing across the street. Members of the press corps remember that some of the whites in the mob began to spray black paint on their camera lenses so that the brutality could not be captured on film. NBC newsman Richard Valeriani was hit in the back of his head with a large club, leaving him bloody and dazed. As Valeriani remembers it, "a white man walked up to me and said, 'Are you hurt? Do you need a doctor?' And I was stunned, and I put my hand to the back of my head and I pulled it back and it was full of blood. And I said to him, 'Yeah, I think I do, I'm bleeding.' And then he thrust his face right up against mine and he said, 'Well, we don't have doctors for people like you.'"[30] In addition to Valeriani, dozens of other people were badly beaten, many requiring hospitalization.

A legion of state troopers began to descend upon the marchers (who were now running for their lives) from every direction. Selma activist Willie Bolden remembers that the sheriff stopped him dead in his tracks, demanding his name. "As I started to tell him what my name was, he put his pistol in my mouth and cocked the trigger, and said 'nigger if you breathe, I'll blow your so-and-so brains out.' When he finally snatched the pistol out of my mouth, he cracked my teeth, hit me up beside my head, and then shouted, 'lock this nigger up.'"[31]

A short distance from where Richard Valeriani and Willie Bolden were being assaulted, a greater tragedy was unfolding. Twenty-six-year-old Jimmie Lee Jackson and his entire family had participated in the march, as had many other local black families in Marion. This kind of activism was nothing new for Jackson, who had been involved in voting rights since he had been denied the right to register four years earlier. The youngest deacon at the St. James Baptist Church in Marion, Jackson had been inspired by the voting rights campaign going on in Selma and had been attending the nightly meetings at Zion United Methodist Church on a regular basis. On this particular night, many of his family members were once again present. As the assault on the marchers continued, Cager Lee, Jimmie Lee Jackson's eighty-two-year-old grandfather, had been beaten and was bleeding profusely. Jackson rushed his grandfather, along with his mother and sister, into Mack's Café, where they were pursued by at least ten Alabama state troopers. Once inside the restaurant, the troopers resumed their attack on Cager Lee, who was offering no resistance and trying in vain to shield himself from their blows. When his daughter Viola stepped in to try to protect her father, troopers began assaulting her. When Jackson intervened to protect his mother, one policeman threw him against a cigarette machine and hit him in the face with his nightstick, while another, James B. Fowler, shot Jackson twice in the stomach at close range. Although severely wounded, Jackson managed to flee the café while being stuck repeatedly by policemen before collapsing in front of the bus station. State troopers continued to beat Jackson while he lay helpless on the ground until they thought he was dead. Barely alive and in critical condition, he was eventually taken to Good Samaritan Hospital in Selma.

Details of the bloodbath in Marion were on the front pages of many of the nation's newspapers the following day. The *Washington Post* ran a banner headline that read "Club-swinging state troopers waded into Negro demonstrators tonight when they marched out of a church to protest voter registration practices. At least 10 Negroes were beaten bloody. Troopers stood by while bystanders beat up cameramen." The headlines of the *New York Times* read "Negroes Beaten in Alabama Riot." Even the *Alabama Journal*, the leading newspaper in Montgomery, decried the assault as "a nightmare of State Police stupidity and brutality." NBC newsman Richard Valeriani appeared on television from his hospital bed, his speech slurred and his head bandaged.

Many SCLC and SNCC activists were convinced that the violence in Marion had only heightened tensions throughout the community, prompting SCLC to temporarily suspend all night marches, which always posed a greater risk of danger. Bernard Lafayette remembers being "absolutely shocked" by the violence in Marion. "In the many earlier marches, there had been beatings and brutalities, but . . . we hadn't anticipated this happening at all. That was a significant turn of events."[32] Meanwhile, on Monday evening, February 22, the Justice Department phoned King to warn him of a possible plot to murder him, which King and his staff had known about for more than a week.

On February 26, eight days after having been shot, Jimmie Lee Jackson died in Good Samaritan Hospital. In the years since his death, new information has come to light suggesting that Jackson's death may have been part of a much wider conspiracy. In a 1979 interview, Dr. William Dinkins (now deceased), one of only two black doctors at Good Samaritan in 1965 and Jimmie Lee Jackson's attending physician, dropped a bombshell. According to Dr. Dinkins, after several days in the hospital, Jackson was "well on the road to recovery. He was sitting up, talking with the nurses, talking with me. His temperature was normal, and all his vitals were good." But just when it appeared that Jackson was out of the woods, Dr. Dinkins remembers that "two white doctors came into his room and suggested that he needed another surgery. I argued against it. I opposed the operation because I didn't think it was necessary; he was alright in my opinion. But being outranked, I eventually gave in." During the surgery, Dr. Dinkins became alarmed when he noticed that Jackson's blood turned from bright red to dark red, indicating insufficient oxygen. "And I called to the anesthetist and said I think you need to put him on 100% oxygen for a while, and the other doctor said I think we need to give him more anesthesia. I said 'no, 100% oxygen.' He said more anesthesia. So he got more anesthesia, and the next thing I knew, he wasn't breathing anymore." Jackson died a short time later, quite possibly from an overdose of anesthesia, but the official cause of death was listed as "peritonitis due to gunshot wound to abdomen." Telling his story fourteen years later, Dr. Dinkins said "Sometimes it's best to pursue things, and sometimes it's best to leave them alone. But at that time, in that particular climate, I thought it was best to leave it alone." [Dr. Dinkins gave this interview to the producers of the highly acclaimed civil rights documentary *Eyes on the Prize*, but it was never used.][33]

Jimmie Lee Jackson's death enraged the black community and almost immediately changed the calculus of the campaign. Albert Turner, a local civil rights activist in Marion, expressed the anger and frustration shared by many: "We were infuriated to the point that we wanted to carry Jimmie's body to George Wallace and dump it on the steps of the Capitol. We had got 'bout like the white folk are. We had determined, or decided that we were going to get killed or we were going to be free. I'm going to be frank about it; a lot of us just about felt that way."[34] Within a few days, the idea of a symbolic march to the statehouse in Montgomery began to catch on. SCLC's Bernard Lafayette remembers that the proposed march "was an important message to those who wanted to retaliate with violence that nonviolence still had power. We needed to show that Jimmie Lee's killing did not stop the movement or discourage people from participation. In fact, it had the reverse effect. . . . We used death as a way to shake people into life, to free those who were paralyzed by fear to understand the value of life."[35]

In fact, it was SCLC's James Bevel who, just two days after Jackson's death, first proposed that protestors take their case directly to Alabama governor George Wallace by marching the entire distance from Selma to the state capital in Montgomery: "I am going to walk all the way from Selma to Montgomery. I have to tell Governor George Wallace what I think about the state troopers who shot Jimmie Lee Jackson."[36] Later that evening, at a mass meeting, Bevel announced his plan to the entire congregation, and then he asked, "How many people are willing to walk with me?" The entire congregation stood. Bevel looked over at Bernard Lafayette, smiled, and then said, "I guess we've got ourselves a march." Thus, the idea of the march from Selma to Montgomery was born.

What had begun in February 1963 as a voter education effort had suddenly been transformed into one of the defining moments of the civil rights movement. The events that had unfolded in Selma, Alabama, and the nearby localities over the past two years provided dramatic evidence that the white power structure would never capitulate, and that only constant pressure, applied by both the civil rights activists and the federal government, could bring about the changes needed that would enfranchise African Americans in the deep South. The marchers would not physically carry Jimmie Lee Jackson's body, but, in a figurative sense, they would carry on their shoulders the weight of the entire movement, including all of the pent-up frustrations and the emotional anguish they had endured collectively over these past many months. The fifty-four-mile trek from Selma to Montgomery, scheduled to begin the following Sunday, would test both the unity of the movement and the participants' commitment to nonviolence.

3

Bloody Sunday

The last thing I remembered seeing on that bridge was this horse running full speed, and this lady, as if in a daze, just stepped right in front of it. The sound of her head hitting that pavement was just too much. You could outrun those state troopers on foot, but you couldn't outrun the ones on horses.

—Joanne Bland, Selma, Alabama, 2008

ON SUNDAY, FEBRUARY 28, a memorial service was held for Jimmie Lee Jackson in Marion, after which there were several meetings in Brown Chapel in Selma. On Monday morning, March 1, King led a march to the courthouse in Selma, telling his followers, "We are going to bring a voting bill into being in the streets of Selma." In Washington, the Justice Department had informed the White House that a voting rights bill focusing on literacy tests and federal registrars was "in the final stages of preparation." While President Johnson seemed to be signaling that he was prepared to move on the issue of voting rights, some inside the White House were more cautious. White House aide Horace Busby was concerned that the proposed elimination of literacy tests would result in white backlash, driving some white moderates into the segregationist camp. What Busby and those of similar mind failed to acknowledge was that such tests had been used not to qualify black voters, but rather to disqualify them, and that *any* remedies supported by the president would come under fire from segregationists.[1]

On Wednesday, March 3, King returned to Selma and spoke at one of two funeral services for Jimmie Lee Jackson, which were attended by a total of more than four thousand people. Mourners draped a large white banner over the entrance to Brown Chapel bearing the words, "Racism Killed Our Brother." Speaking at the service, King said that Jackson "was murdered by the irresponsibility of every politician from governors on down who have fed his constituents the stale bread of hatred and the spoiled meat of racism. He was murdered by the timidity of a federal government that can spend millions of dollars a day to keep troops in South Vietnam and cannot protect the lives of its own citizens seeking the right to vote. . . . And by every Negro who passively accepts the evils of segregation and stands on the sidelines in the struggle for justice."[2] Later that evening, James Bevel told the press that the march from Selma to Montgomery would begin on Sunday, March 7, and that Dr. King would lead it.

On Thursday, March 4, Governor Wallace met with Alabama public safety director Al Lingo and his staff for several hours to discuss how they would handle Sunday's march. In his later account of that meeting, Wallace's press secretary Bill Jones asserted that he, Jones, had suggested that the marchers, who expected to be blocked, be allowed to march along U.S. Highway 80 toward Montgomery. Unbeknownst to the marchers, however, the highway would be closed to *all* vehicular traffic except that of local residents. With no support vehicles and inadequate supplies, the marchers, or so Jones believed, would not get very far, and that press coverage would be greatly minimized: "When the conference finally ended . . . Wallace was sold on the idea of letting them march. I did not believe—nor did any of us who were present—that King and his fellow travelers could march the 50 miles to Montgomery. I firmly believed my plan could make them the laughing stock of the nation and win for us a propaganda battle."[3] But later that day, Wallace was told that if the marchers somehow managed to make it as far as Lowndes County (nicknamed "Bloody Lowndes"), which had a notorious reputation for racial violence, the marchers would likely encounter explosives or shootings. According to Jones, this ominous prediction caused Wallace to change his mind about allowing the marchers to proceed. At a later meeting, Wallace, Lingo, and state trooper majors John Cloud and William R. Jones discussed their strategies for halting the marchers.

While Wallace and Lingo were strategizing in Montgomery, back in Selma Mayor Smitherman, who had received assurances from the governor's staff that the plan was to stop the march peacefully, was having a difficult time convincing his public safety director, Wilson Baker, that there would be no violence. Baker suspected that Lingo and Sheriff Clark were planning a blood-bath on Sunday, and he had shared his concerns with the mayor on at least two occasions. But Smitherman continued to repeat the reassurances he had been given by the governor's staff. Still, Baker was so concerned about the potential for violence that he reportedly threatened to resign. Hearing of Baker's concerns, several of Selma's city council members gave assurances that the city police, over whom Baker technically had jurisdiction, would not interfere with the marchers.

Wilson Baker was not the only one who was concerned about the potential for violence. SNCC, the civil rights organization with the longest history in Selma, tried to convince SCLC not to proceed with the march. Citing their concerns about the potential for violence, SNCC had opposed the march from the outset and had voted that the organization would not participate. In a letter to King, John Lewis explained SNCC's rationale: "We strongly believe that the objectives of the march do not justify the dangers . . . consequently, the Student Nonviolent Coordinating Committee will [only] live up to those minimal commitments . . . to provide radios and cars, doctors and nurses, and nothing beyond that."[4] SNCC's executive secretary James Forman later summarized the organization's position: "Basically SNCC was opposed to a Selma–Montgomery march because of the likelihood of police brutality, the drain on resources, and the frustrations experienced in working with SCLC."[5]

Ever since SNCC's founding in April 1960, the organization had engaged in friendly competition with SCLC, and over time, some tension between the two groups had emerged. In fact, there had always been some degree of tension between all of the major civil rights organizations, as they often competed for the same limited pool of resources. But owing to differences over strategy and leadership, and what many suspect was SNCC's increasing jealousy of Martin Luther King's star power, the relationship between these two groups in particular had soured. Even though SNCC had voted not to formally participate in Sunday's march, it was agreed that SNCC members who wanted to march, such as John Lewis, would be permitted to do so, not as representatives of SNCC, but as private citizens.

On Friday, March 5, King and President Johnson met for a little over an hour, and White House records indicate that the two discussed a wide range of subjects. Afterwards King told reporters that he had made clear to the president that any voting rights legislation had to include the use of federal registrars to ensure compliance and the abolition of literacy tests, although King said that the president had made no promises. However, on the very day of their meeting, the Justice Department completed draft legislation that called for an end to literacy tests and the use of federal registrars, but under certain conditions. As proposed, literacy tests would have to be suspended in all states and subdivisions that used them *and* that had registration *or* turnout levels that fell below 50 percent of the voting-age population in 1964. This would eliminate all literacy tests in Alabama, Mississippi, Louisiana, Georgia, South Carolina, Virginia, and Alaska, as well as in several dozen North Carolina counties and some other counties across the nation. Although this formula would not affect certain "problem" counties in Arkansas, Florida, Tennessee, and Texas, the Justice Department acknowledged that its primary goal was to focus on the "hard-core" problem areas. As for federal registrars, the attorney general had the authority to appoint them for any locality where literacy tests had been suspended. Anyone convicted of trying to prevent a registered voter from voting faced five years in prison and a $5,000 fine.[6]

Saturday, March 6, began with a statement from Governor George Wallace prohibiting the march from Selma to Montgomery on the grounds that such a venture would pose a threat to public safety: "Such action would not be allowed on the part of any other group of citizens or non-citizens of the state of Alabama, and will not be allowed in this instance. Government must proceed in an orderly manner, and lawful and law-abiding citizens must transact their business with the government in such a manner. There will be no march between Selma, Alabama, and Montgomery, and I have so instructed the Department of Public Safety."[7]

Also on that Saturday, about seventy sympathetic whites marched to the Dallas County Courthouse where their leader, the Rev. Joseph Ellwanger, read a statement that was largely drowned out by the taunts and jeers of roughly one hundred hostile whites. A native of Selma and chairman of the Concerned White Citizens of Alabama, Ellwanger said that he and his group had "come to Selma today to tell the nation that there are white people in Alabama who will speak out against the events which have recently occurred in this and neighboring counties and towns. We consider it a shocking injustice that there are still counties in Alabama where there are no Negroes registered to vote and where Negroes have reason to fear hostility and harassment by public officials when they do try to register . . . We are horrified at the brutal way in which the police at times have attempted to break up peaceful assemblies and demonstrations by American citizens who are exercising their constitutional right to protest injustice . . ."[8]

As Ellwanger continued to speak, the large group of segregationists who had gathered tried to drown him out by singing "Dixie." Ellwanger and his group responded by singing "America the Beautiful." Some African Americans who had been drawn to the scene began singing "We Shall Overcome." Fearing that violence would soon break out, Wilson Baker rushed to the courthouse and urged Ellwanger and his group to leave. They complied, as did the blacks who were at the scene, but not before the segregationists had attacked a SNCC photographer. When the man managed to lock himself in a parked car, the mob hoisted the vehicle off the ground, but Baker persuaded them to put the car down without harming the photographer.[9]

There was yet another interesting development on that Saturday. Despite his earlier promise to lead the march, King decided at the last minute to remain in Atlanta on Sunday to fulfill what he said were his pastoral obligations to his church. King had served as the pastor of Dexter Avenue Baptist Church in Montgomery from 1954 until 1960, when he resigned the pulpit because of his increasing civil rights activism. Since then, he had served as co-pastor of his home church, Ebenezer Baptist Church in Atlanta, along with his father, Rev. Martin Luther King, Sr. King and his father, known affectionately as "Daddy King," alternated preaching on the first Sunday of each month, which was when Ebenezer observed communion. It was King's turn to preach, and he chose to honor that commitment. King's closest confidante, the Rev. Ralph David Abernathy, served as pastor of West Hunter Baptist Church, and he also remained in Atlanta to conduct his service. But King's noticeable absence from the march he had promised to lead would be the source of much controversy and speculation for years to come.[10]

In addition to not wanting to break his preaching commitment at Ebenezer, King later offered other explanations for his decision not to participate in Sunday's march. In an essay he published just weeks later, King wrote that "none of us anticipated [or even] imagined that they would use the brutal methods to which they actually resorted." And in a statement he apparently offered to the press later in the evening of March 7, King said "he and staff members of the Southern Christian Leadership Conference . . . had agreed last night [Saturday, March 6] that he should not lead the march because they had learned troopers would block it." King also said that while he expected that there would be mass arrests, he was not expecting any serious violence. However, the fact that ten doctors and nurses had flown in to Selma from New York that Saturday, along with the presence of several ambulances, strongly suggests that someone was expecting violence. No doubt, King was aware of these developments. His explanations notwithstanding, it is very likely that King either decided himself—or was persuaded by SCLC staffers—to absent himself from the march *because* of the likelihood of violence. Two chroniclers of movement events suggest that King avoided the march because of the personal danger it posed to him. Paul Good later wrote, "Dr. King had been advised by Attorney General Katzenbach not to take part," and Jim Bishop wrote that King had told his wife "that he had not led the march because he had been warned there was a plot to kill him in the melee." Given the violence that had occurred in Selma up to that point, King had good reason to be concerned for his physical safety.[11]

John Lewis offered up yet another version that provides a somewhat contradictory sequence of events that explains King's absence. As Lewis remembered it, King still wanted to lead the march, but he wanted to postpone it until Monday. He had apparently decided Saturday evening that he needed to be at Ebenezer that Sunday and that the march would have to be postponed until Monday. Lewis recalled seeing Andrew Young, Hosea Williams, and James Bevel huddled together just a few hours before the march, talking to each other in an animated discussion. Apparently, Young had just learned of King's decision, and he was now informing Williams and Bevel, neither of whom was pleased with this turn of events. They decided on the spot that with hundreds of people already gathered, there was simply no way to call off the march. When he saw that the march could not be stopped, Young went inside the church to call King in Atlanta. King apparently gave in, and then instructed Young to choose one among them to co-lead the march along with Lewis. The other two would remain behind to handle logistics just in case there was trouble. This version of events, of course, begs the question what did SCLC staffers know about King's decision not to be in Selma on Sunday, and when did they know it. But regardless of what version one believes, it is apparent that for whatever reason, King had changed his mind about proceeding with the march on Sunday, and it is unlikely that his decision was influenced solely by his pastoral obligations, which he most certainly would have known of well in advance.[12]

On the morning of the march, Sunday, March 7, SCLC lieutenants Andrew Young, Hosea Williams, and James Bevel met at Brown Chapel and flipped a coin to decide who would lead the march in King's absence. Hosea Williams won the toss (or, as he would joke years later, he actually "lost" the toss) and would co-lead the march; movement veteran John Lewis, who had been arrested and beaten many times in his activist career, would walk beside Williams. Although technically marching as a private citizen, his position as SNCC's national chairman could hardly be ignored. Throughout the day marchers had been assembling at Brown Chapel, many of them coming straight from church and wearing their Sunday best. Many of the men were dressed in suits and ties, and many of the women were wearing high heels. Earlier in the day SCLC veterans had held impromptu training sessions, teaching people how to protect their bodies if they were beaten. They were told to wet their handkerchiefs so that they could use them to cover their eyes and noses if they were tear-gassed. Last but not least, they were all told that no matter what happened on the march, they were to remain true to the principles of nonviolence. Meanwhile, a team of doctors and nurses from a New York–based group called the Medical Committee for Human Rights had set up a makeshift clinic in the small parsonage beside the church.

It was close to 4:00 p.m. when Andrew Young, Hosea Williams, James Bevel, and John Lewis gathered the marchers, who by now numbered nearly six hundred. A dozen or so reporters were also present. After John Lewis read a short statement aloud for the benefit of the press, explaining the purpose of the march, the marchers knelt and bowed their heads as Andrew Young delivered a prayer. And then they set out to walk across the long arched edifice known as the Edmund Pettus Bridge (named after a Confederate general and Grand Dragon of the Ku Klux Klan) that crossed the Alabama River and led out of Selma toward Montgomery. Included in their ranks was a white SCLC staffer named Al Lingo—ironically a name shared by the commander of Alabama's state troopers.

They walked in a double column, two abreast, in a pair of lines that stretched for several blocks. "I can't count the number of marches I have participated in in my lifetime," recalled John Lewis, "but there was something peculiar about this one. It was more than disciplined. It was somber and sub-dued, almost like a funeral procession. No one was jostling or pushing to get to the front . . . I don't know if there was a feeling that something was going to happen, or if the people simply sensed that this was a special procession, a 'leaderless' march. There were no big names up front, no celebrities. This was just plain folks moving through the streets of Selma." Walking behind Williams and Lewis were SCLC leaders Albert Turner from Perry County and Bob Mants from Lowndes County. They were followed by veteran school teacher Amelia Boynton and Marie Foster, a local dental assistant. Behind them, stretching as far as the eye could see, walked an army of teenagers, teachers, undertakers, beauticians, Selma's rank and file—many of the same people who had for years, and in vain, tried to register to vote. Bringing up the rear were four slow-moving ambulances that were not allowed to follow the marchers onto the bridge.[13]

"When we reached the crest of the bridge, I stopped dead still," remem-bers Lewis. "So did Hosea. There, facing us at the bottom of the other side, stood a sea of blue-helmeted, blue-uniformed Alabama state troopers, line after line of them, dozens of battle-ready lawmen stretched from one side of U.S. Highway 80 to the other. Behind them were several dozen more armed men—Sheriff Clark's posse—some on horseback, all wearing khaki clothing, many carrying clubs the size of baseball bats. . . . It was a drop of one hundred feet from the top of that bridge to the river below. Hosea glanced down at the muddy water and said, 'Can you swim?' 'No,' I answered. 'Well,' he said, with a tiny half smile, 'neither can I. . . . But we might have to.'"[14]

As the marchers moved closer, some of the troopers began slipping their gas masks over their faces. At the bottom of the bridge, while the marchers were still about fifty feet from the troopers, Major John Cloud stepped for-ward, holding a small bullhorn up to his mouth. Williams and Lewis stopped in their tracks, as did everyone else who was close enough to see what was happening. "This is an unlawful assembly," Cloud said. "Your march is not conducive to the public safety. You are ordered to disperse and go back to your church or to your homes." A wave of numbing anxiety swept across the marchers at this point and they remained frozen in their tracks, paralyzed either by fear or indecision. Williams then asked, "May we have a word with the major?" to which Cloud replied, "There is no word to be had." Williams then repeated the question and got the same response. Cloud then issued his final warning: "You have two minutes to turn around and go back to your church."[15]

Bernard Lafayette perhaps said it best when, reflecting years later, he wrote that "Hosea Williams and John Lewis were the two most unlikely persons to obey such a command. This confrontation was not their first, nor would it be their last. They shared a common spirit of being nonviolent battering rams and threw the weight of their souls against this violent confrontation." As John Lewis put it, "I wasn't about to turn around. We were there. We were not going to run. We couldn't turn back and go back even if we wanted to. There were too many people." While not wanting to retreat, Lewis also clearly understood the dangers of going forward, and did not want to do anything that would provoke the troopers. As he saw it, the only option they had at that moment was to kneel in prayer. Williams and Lewis knelt down in prayer, as did the other marchers behind them. As Lewis began to pray out loud, the troopers lined up and prepared themselves for battle, putting on their gas masks and pulling out their nightsticks. Lewis may have thought they had two minutes, but they did not. "One minute after he had issued his warning—I know this because I was careful to check my watch—Major Cloud issued an order to his troopers. "Troopers," he shouted, "Advance." It was 4:15 p.m. And then all hell broke loose.[16]

Roy Reed, a reporter for the *New York Times*, described the chaos he witnessed that day:

The troopers rushed forward, their blue uniforms and white helmets blurring into a flying wedge as they moved. The wedge moved with such force that it seemed almost to pass over the waiting column instead of through it. The first 10 or 20 Negroes were swept to the ground screaming, arms and legs flying, and packs and bags went skittering across the grassy divider strip and on to the pavement on both sides. Those still on their feet retreated. The troopers continued pushing, using both the force of their bodies and the prodding of their nightsticks. A cheer went up from the white spectators lining the south side of the highway. The mounted possemen spurred their horses and rode at a run into the retreating mass. The Negroes cried out as they crowded together for protection, and the whites on the sidelines whooped and cheered. The Negroes paused in their retreat for perhaps a minute, still screaming and huddling together. Suddenly there was a report like a gunshot and a grey cloud spewed over the troopers

On "Bloody Sunday," March 7, 1965, scores of marchers were brutally assaulted on the Edmund Pettus Bridge as they attempted to march from Selma to Montgomery. Many of the marchers sustained cuts and bruises, severe head gashes, fractured arms and ribs, broken teeth, tear gas burns, and at least one fractured skull—suffered by John Lewis. Here, a policeman stands over one of the female marchers after she had been beaten, while other troopers sit on their horses nearby assessing the carnage. Prints and Photographs Division, Library of Congress

and the Negroes. "Tear gas," someone yelled. The cloud began covering the highway. Newsmen, who were confined by four troopers to a corner 100 yards away, began to lose sight of the action. But before the cloud finally hid it all, there were several seconds of unobstructed view. Fifteen or twenty nightsticks could be seen through the gas, flailing at the heads of the marchers. The Negroes broke and ran. Scores of them streamed across the parking lot of the Selma Tractor Company. Troopers and possemen, mounted and unmounted, went after them.[17]

John Lewis remembers it this way:

The troopers and possemen swept forward as one, like a human wave, a blur of blue shirts and billy clubs and bullwhips. We had no chance to turn and retreat. There were six hundred people behind us, bridge railings to either side, and the river below. I remember how vivid the sounds were as the troopers rushed toward us—the clunk of the troopers' heavy boots, the whoops of rebel yells from the white onlookers, the clip-clop of horses' hooves hitting the hard asphalt of the highway, the voice of a woman shouting, "Get 'em. *Get* the niggers!" And then they were upon us. The first of the troopers came over me, a large, husky man. Without a word, he swung his club against the left side of my head. I didn't feel any pain, just the thud of the blow, and my legs giving way. . . . And then the same trooper hit me again. And everything started to spin. I heard something that sounded like gunshots. And then a cloud of smoke rose all around us. Tear gas. I'd never experienced tear gas before. This, I would learn later, was a particularly toxic form called C-4, made to induce nausea. I began choking, coughing. I couldn't get air into my lungs. I felt as if I was taking my last breath. If there was ever a time in my life for me to panic, it should have been then. But I didn't. I remember how strangely calm I felt as I thought, This is it. People are going to die here. *I'm* going to die here. . . . I was bleeding badly. My head was now exploding with pain. . . . There was mayhem all around me. I could see a young kid—a teenaged boy—sitting on the ground with a gaping cut in his head, the blood just gushing out. Several women, including Mrs. Boynton, were lying on the pavement and the grass median. People were weeping. Some were vomiting from the tear gas. Men on horses were moving in all directions, purposely riding over the fallen people, bringing their animals' hooves down on shoulders, stomachs and legs. The mob of white onlookers had joined in now, jumping cameramen and reporters.[18]

Selma resident and civil rights activist Joanne Bland was eleven years old in 1965, and she, along with her fourteen-year-old sister, Linda, were on that bridge on "Bloody Sunday." As she remembers it:

We were near the back of the line, but we could hear all the terror going on down front. Then we heard shots, and thought they were killing the people. We soon learned that what we thought were gunshots were tear gas canisters exploding, and that cloud of smoke was suffocating the people. Tear gas gets in your eyes, it burns your eyes and burns your lungs. You can't see. And then you panic. Oftentimes you run right back into the same people

As the marchers struggled to collect their wits after the vicious beatings, Alabama state troopers added to the chaos by using tear gas on the peaceful protestors. Since the marchers had already started back across the bridge once the police began the assault with their nightsticks, it was evident that the troopers used the gas not to disperse the marchers, but to cause further injury and panic. Disoriented, gasping for air, and blinded in the cloud of burning gas, some of the marchers ran directly into the path of oncoming horses. Prints and Photographs Division, Library of Congress

you're running from. It was awful. Blood was everywhere on that bridge. They were running horses up in the crowd, and the horses were afraid; and they would rear up, and when they came down, it was no place for you to go. In fact, the last thing I remembered seeing on that bridge was this horse running full speed, and this lady, as if in a daze, just stepped right in front of it. The sound of her head hitting that pavement was just too much. You could outrun those state troopers on foot, but you couldn't outrun the ones on horses. I fainted. And when I awoke I was in a car on the bridge. And my sister Linda was in that car, and she was just crying. And when I became fully awake I realized that it was not her tears falling on my face, it was her blood. My fourteen-year-old sister had been beaten on that bridge, and had a wound in her head that required eighteen stitches.[19]

"The horses . . . were more humane than the troopers; they stepped over fallen victims," recalled Amelia Boynton. "As I stepped aside from a trooper's club, I felt a blow on my arm . . . Another blow by a trooper, as I was gasping for breath, knocked me to the ground and there I lay, unconscious . . . ." Shey-ann Webb, then eight years old, remembers "All I could remember was out-bursts of tear gas, and I saw people being beaten, and I just tried to run home as fast as I could. And as I began to run home I saw horses behind me; and I will never forget, a freedom fighter picked me up—Hosea Williams—and I told him to put me down, he wasn't running fast enough." Andrew Young remembers that "we were about two blocks away from the bridge, and we went back to try to help people. But the police were riding along on horseback beating people . . . The tear gas was so thick you couldn't get to where the people were who needed help. And so we really had to turn the church into a hospital just to get people back to their senses. And it was a horrible two or three hours." Long after the others had fled the scene of the initial attack, five black women were still lying on the bridge. The ambulances had not been allowed to follow the marchers on the bridge, and the women, who had been unconscious but were eventually roused by further tear gassing, eventually made it back safely across the bridge into Selma.[20]

The raw terror that had occurred on the Edmund Pettus Bridge stunned the nation. The scenes of shocking brutality made their way into the homes of millions of television viewers as the major networks interrupted their regular programming to show video footage of what would become known as "Bloody Sunday." ABC broke into its broadcast of the film *Judgment at Nuremberg* (a film about Nazi war crimes). News anchor Frank Reynolds came on screen to tell viewers of the violent beatings that black protest marchers in Selma had endured at the hands of Alabama state troopers. The network aired fifteen minutes of film footage from the attack. "When that beating happened at the foot of the bridge, it looked like war," Selma mayor Smitherman recalled many years later. "That [video footage] went all over the country. And the people, the wrath of the nation came down on us." All these years later, John Lewis still finds it hard to comprehend what happened on the bridge that day. "The images were stunning—scene after scene of policemen on foot and on horseback beating defenseless American citizens. Many viewers thought this was somehow part of the movie. It seemed too strange, too ugly to be real. It *couldn't* be real." At one point in the film clip, Sheriff Clark's voice could be heard clearly in the background: "Get those goddamned niggers!" he yelled. "And get those goddamned *white* niggers."[21]

While the beatings that occurred on the bridge are generally well known and have been well documented over the years, another, far more brutal dimension of "Bloody Sunday" has not received significant attention, mainly because there were fewer journalists to cover it as well as a concerted effort by police authorities to conceal it—and that is that the beatings of the marchers and other Selma residents, some of whom had taken no part in the march, continued well into the night of March 7. As the marchers began to retreat across the bridge, the state troopers and possemen were in hot pursuit and were joined by white onlookers. Both on foot and on horseback, the troopers and possemen chased any blacks they could find into downtown Selma and then into the black neighborhood and housing project adjacent to Brown Chapel. One of the few people present that night with a camera was a white man who was viciously attacked and had his camera taken away. That man turned out to be an FBI agent who was mistaken for a journalist, and the three men who attacked him were later arrested—one of whom was Jimmie George Robinson, the same man who had attacked Dr. King a couple of months earlier when King had registered as the first ever black guest at the Hotel Albert in Selma.

John Lewis remembers that as the marchers headed back toward Selma, the troopers and possemen pursued them with nightsticks and whips. "One posseman had a rubber hose wrapped with barbed wire. Sheriff Clark's 'deputies' chased us all the way back into the Carver project and up to the front of Brown Chapel, where we tried getting as many people as we could inside the church to safety. I don't even recall how I made it that far, how I got from the bridge to the church, but I did." A United Press International reporter provided this account of the bloody nightmare that continued until well after dark: "The troopers and possemen, under Gov. George Wallace's orders to stop the Negroes' 'Walk for Freedom' from Selma to Montgomery, chased the screaming, bleeding marchers nearly a mile back to their church, clubbing them as they ran. Ambulances screamed in relays between Good Samaritan Hospital and Brown Chapel Church, carrying hysterical men, women, and children suffering head wounds and tear gas burns."[22]

At least 150 troopers and possemen, including Clark himself, kept up the attack for hours, beating anyone who remained on the street. Eventually, however, shock gave way to anger, and some of the blacks began to fight back, with men and boys emerging from the Carver homes with bottles and bricks in their hands, throwing them at the troopers. Further up Sylvan Street, troopers chased a group of blacks into the First Baptist Church. But even after they had managed to get inside the church, they still were not safe. Troopers fired tear gas inside the church, and once inside they beat a teenaged boy and threw him through one of the church's windows. It was not until Public Safety Director Wilson Baker arrived some time later that Clark and his men were persuaded to retreat to a distance of one block from Brown Chapel, but still Clark and his men refused to leave the Sylvan Street area. Angry blacks from the neighborhood then gathered in front of the church; some teenagers continued to throw bottles and bricks while some men in the crowd began to talk of going home to get their guns. But SCLC and SNCC staffers began to move through the crowd trying to defuse what was already an explosive situation.[23]

Only when calm was finally restored could movement staffers turn their attention to those who had been beaten and bloodied. The parsonage next to the church had quite literally been converted to a hospital, with doctors and nurses treating the injured. Among the many injuries the victims sustained were cuts and bruises, severe head gashes, fractured ribs and arms, broken teeth, tear gas burns, and at least one fractured skull—suffered by John Lewis. The most seriously injured were taken to Good Samaritan Hospital, Selma's largest black healthcare facility. Operated by Catholics and staffed mostly by black doctors and nurses, it was also the place where Jimmie Lee Jackson had died from his gunshot wounds. Because of the number of wounded, the four ambulances were not nearly sufficient for the task of transporting the injured to the hospital, so several local black funeral homes offered their hearses to be used for that purpose. One of those ambulance drivers made ten trips back and forth from the hospital to the church and to nearby Burwell Infirmary, a smaller clinic. More than ninety men, women, and children were treated at both facilities.[24]

Despite the severity of his injuries, John Lewis refused to seek medical attention immediately. Although several people were trying to convince him that he needed to go to the hospital, Lewis wanted to remain at the church, doing what he could to calm and reassure the others. Once things began to settle down, SCLC staffers decided to call a mass meeting at the church, and more than six hundred people—many bandaged from the wounds they had received that day—attended. Sheriff Clark's posse had been ordered to leave, but the state troopers remained on the scene.

Hosea Williams spoke to the crowd first. Then, as Lewis recalls, he stood to speak next, but his head was throbbing, his hair was matted with blood, and his trench coat was stained with dirt and blood. Shaky and unsteady, he looked out over the mass gathering, "crammed wall to wall and floor to ceiling with people. There was not a spot for one more body." With no speech prepared, and having no idea what to say, the words just came: "I don't know how President Johnson can send troops to Vietnam. I don't see how he can send troops to the Congo. I don't see how he can send troops to *Africa*, and he can't send troops to Selma, Alabama." The crowd clapped and cheered, and several shouted "Yes!" and "Amen!" "Next time we march," Lewis continued, "we may have to keep going when we get to Montgomery. We may have to go on to *Washington*." When those words were printed in the *New York Times* the next morning, the Justice Department announced it was sending FBI agents to Selma to investigate whether "unnecessary force was used by law officers and others." Lewis later reflected that "For two months we'd been facing 'unnecessary force,' but that apparently had not been enough. This, finally, was enough." After finishing his speech, Lewis consented to go next door to the parsonage to have his injuries attended to. The doctors took one look at his head and immediately sent him to Good Samaritan Hospital.[25]

Monday, March 8, was a day of sober reflection, and many thought they were awakening from a terrible nightmare. "We saw the news footage the next day," said John Lewis. Still, it was hard to comprehend what the images had made so clear. "People just couldn't believe this was happening, not in America. Women and children being attacked by armed men on horseback—it was impossible to believe." But as civil rights activists reflected many years later, they were convinced that there was something very different about the beating on the Edmund Pettus Bridge, something more bizarre and more sinister. To be sure, there had already been too much violence and too many murders—Bull Connor's police dogs being turned loose on children in Birmingham in 1963; the dynamite explosion in the 16th Street Baptist Church in Birmingham a few months later that claimed the lives of four little girls; the murders of Chaney, Goodman, and Schwerner in Mississippi during "Freedom Summer" in 1964. But something about that day in Selma touched a nerve deeper than anything that had come before. "This wasn't like Birmingham, where chanting and cheering and singing preceded a wild stampede and scattering," remembers John Lewis. "This was a face-off in the most vivid terms between a dignified, composed, completely nonviolent multitude of silent protestors and the truly malevolent force of a heavily armed, hateful battalion of troopers. The sight of them rolling over us like human tanks was something that had never been seen before."[26]

Even before the smoke from the tear gas had completely cleared, people from all across the nation had begun to descend upon Selma, Alabama. People from as far away as New York, Minnesota, and California were flying and driving into Selma, some keeping vigil outside Brown Chapel. Having been kept apprised of the situation by the Justice Department, President Johnson had seen the footage and he knew he would have to respond. Andrew Young had notified Dr. King in Atlanta almost immediately, and King was now more determined than ever that there *would* be a march. First thing Monday morning, SCLC asked for a federal injunction barring state interference in a Selma to Montgomery march. That request arrived in Montgomery, and landed on the desk of Federal District judge Frank Johnson—the same judge who had issued an injunction in 1961 granting the "Freedom Riders" safe passage out of Montgomery.

"Bloody Sunday" was a defining moment in the black freedom struggle. The police brutality that occurred on the Edmund Pettus Bridge—all captured on film—was unlike anything that had previously been seen in America. The state troopers' total disregard for human life and for the lawful rights of American citizens was on full display for the world to see, as the constitutional liberties and protections guaranteed to African Americans were literally trampled beneath horses' hooves. Movement leaders would have to regroup for the next phase of this campaign, and would have to mobilize people of all persuasions all over the country to use this tragic episode to arouse the conscience of a nation.

4

My Feets is tired, but my Soul is rested

What happened in Selma is part of a far larger movement which reaches into every section and State of America. It is the effort of American Negroes to secure for themselves the full blessings of American life. Their cause must be our cause too. Because it is not just Negroes, but really it is all of us, who must overcome the crippling legacy of bigotry and injustice. And we *shall* overcome.

—President Lyndon B. Johnson, Address to Joint Session of Congress, March 15, 1965

ON THE EVENING OF MARCH 7, as Alabama state troopers and Sheriff Jim Clark's posse were still patrolling the streets of Selma looking for people to beat up, Martin Luther King busied himself in Atlanta sending telegrams to prominent clergymen across the nation. "In the vicious mal-treatment of defenseless citizens of Selma," King wrote, "where old women and young children were gassed and clubbed at random, we have witnessed an eruption of the disease of racism which seeks to destroy all America. No American is without responsibility. . . . Join me in Selma for a ministers' march to Montgomery on Tuesday morning, March 9." In Montgomery, an unapologetic Governor Wallace declared that "Those folks in Selma have made this a seven-day-a-week job, but we can't give one inch. We're going to enforce state law." Selma's Mayor Smitherman, equally unmoved by the day's events, tried to discredit King, saying that the occurrence on the Edmund Pettus Bridge should make it "evident to the Negro people . . . that King and the other leaders who ask them to break the law are always absent from the violence as he was today."[1]

On Capitol Hill on Monday, March 8, six members of the House of Representatives and the Senate reacted publicly to the news of the previous afternoon's attack. New York Senator Jacob Javits referred to the violence as "an exercise in terror," and the others had harsh words for the tactics used by the Alabama lawmen, with several of them aiming their strongest criticism at Governor Wallace. Texas senator Ralph Yarborough was blunt: "Shame on you George Wallace, for the wet ropes that bruised the muscles, for the bull-whips that cut the flesh, for the clubs that broke the bones, and for the tear gas that seared the eyes and the nose and the nostrils and the lungs, and choked people into insensibility. This is *not* the American way." Walter Mondale of Minnesota concluded, "Sunday's outrage in Selma, Alabama, makes passage of legislation to guarantee Southern Negroes the right to vote an absolute imperative for Congress this year."[2]

King returned to Selma on Monday, March 8, the day after Bloody Sunday, facing a new crisis. Governor Wallace had made it clear that there would be no marches between Selma and Montgomery, and SCLC had asked U.S. District Court Judge Frank M. Johnson to prevent Governor Wallace from interfering with Tuesday's march. But Judge Johnson did not honor their request, saying that he would not do so without a hearing, and that the earliest he could hold such a hearing would be that Thursday. On Monday afternoon the question of whether to go ahead with the Tuesday march dominated an almost continuous twelve-hour-long series of discussions, held at the home of local black dentist, Dr. Sullivan Jackson. Present along with King at the meetings were SCLC staffers Ralph Abernathy, Andrew Young, and Hosea Williams, among others. SNCC was represented by its executive secretary James Forman, Willie Ricks, and Fay Bellamy. James Farmer, president of CORE (Congress of Racial Equality) was also present, as were several attorneys, led by Fred Gray, who had represented Rosa Parks during the Montgomery Bus Boycott. The central issue was whether they should risk losing Judge Johnson's support by proceeding with the march before getting his approval, or risk losing credibility and the movement's momentum by waiting.

The group was almost evenly divided. Although he had been dead set against Sunday's march, James Forman of SNCC was pushing hard for the march to take place on Tuesday, and was clearly not in the mood to postpone. Hosea Williams agreed, fearing that the spirit and the momentum of the campaign might be lost if they didn't march on Tuesday. At the very least, Williams argued, they owed it to those whose heads had been busted open and whose eyes and nostrils had been seared with tear gas on the Pettus Bridge the day before. But after hours of debate, the final decision ultimately rested with King: the march would be postponed until some official word from Judge Johnson.

Following the meeting, the movement leaders proceeded to Brown Chapel for a midnight rally. The church was packed with people, including many who had just recently arrived in Selma after having seen news footage of the previous day's assault on the bridge. Clearly overwhelmed by the turnout of more than a thousand people and the emotional atmosphere (and perhaps for the first time fully comprehending the arguments that Forman and Williams had been making), King stunned everyone when he rose and announced to the crowd that there *would* be a march the next day. "We've gone too far to turn back now," King said. "We must let them know that nothing can stop us—not even death itself. We must be ready for a season of suffering. The only way we can achieve freedom is to conquer the fear of death. Man dies when he refuses to stand up for what is right, for what is just, for what is true," King concluded. There would be a march tomorrow, and this time King would lead it.[3]

King, however, was not totally comfortable with that decision, and he was being pressured by White House officials not to go through with it. SCLC and SNCC staffers who favored the march and those who opposed it continued their heated discussions for the next several hours at Dr. Jackson's home. King finally went to bed at around 4:00 a.m., but sometime around 5:00 a.m. he was awakened by a phone call from Attorney General Katzenbach who conveyed to King that it was President Johnson's wish that the march be called off. After a few hours' sleep, King met with several federal officials, including John Doar from the Justice Department and former Florida governor LeRoy Collins, who was now the director of the Justice Department's Community Relations Service. Doar made it clear to King that Judge Frank Johnson would hand down an order barring any march on Tuesday unless he received word that SCLC would not proceed with the march. Knowing full well the ramifications of disobeying a federal judge's order, King was in a tight spot, and Attorney General Katzenbach sensed that King was looking for an honorable exit strategy. Still unable to dissuade King, Collins indicated that he would meet with Colonel Lingo and Sheriff Clark to try to work out some kind of arrangement.[4]

Collins met with Lingo and Clark in the office of a car dealership on U.S. 80 near the location of Sunday's attack. Collins told them of King's determination to march, and Lingo and Clark replied that they would not permit the march to occur. Collins then asked if a physical confrontation could be avoided if the marchers turned around upon reaching the officers' line, to which both Lingo and Clark replied yes. Collins then communicated this to King, who apparently was noncommittal, although Collins believed that King had accepted the compromise. Collins then returned to Lingo and Clark and told them that he believed a confrontation could be avoided.

By mid-morning on Tuesday, March 9, Judge Johnson had issued a restraining order barring any march prior to the hearing, after reportedly having been told by Collins that no formal decision on postponing the march had been made. Meanwhile at Brown Chapel, people were beginning to stream in and various speakers were proclaiming their right to march, despite the judge's order, which by then had been served on several SCLC staffers. At 2:30 p.m. King arrived at the church and announced that he was ready to march. Tension, excitement, and anxiety filled the air, and many in the crowd began to sing freedom songs to steel their nerves. At around 3:00 p.m. King addressed the crowd. "We have the right to walk the highways, and we have the right to walk to Montgomery if our feet will get us there," he said. "I have no alternative but to lead a march from this spot to carry our grievances to the seat of government. I have to march," to which cheers and applause erupted. "I do not know what lies ahead of us. There may be beatings, jailing, tear gas. But I would rather die on the highways of Alabama than make a butchery of my conscience. There is nothing more tragic in all this world than to know right and not to do it."[5] Within a few minutes the column of roughly two thousand marchers formed and began to move out.

The marchers then began their trek out of Selma, following the same route they had taken two days earlier. As the column reached the foot of the Pettus Bridge shortly after 3:00 p.m. they were stopped by Stanley Fountain, chief deputy marshal of the Southern District of Alabama, who read aloud Judge Johnson's order, which the marchers assumed was a mere formality. When King indicated that he intended to proceed, the marshal stepped aside. As the marchers descended the other side of the bridge, once again they came face to face with Major John Cloud and the wall of state troopers. LeRoy Collins had promised King that if the marchers turned around once they got to the other side of the bridge, there would be no bloody confrontation. But King remained uneasy, not sure whether Colonel Lingo and Sheriff Clark would be able to restrain themselves. Nor was he sure that he would be able to control his own followers, some of whom might refuse to turn around.

As he had on Sunday, Major Cloud told the marchers, "You are ordered to stop and stand where you are. This march will not continue." The show of police force was even more imposing than it had been on Bloody Sunday. Major Cloud's state troopers were backed up by Sheriff Clark's posse, and an additional 150 carloads of troopers, five hundred in all, had been added to the existing force. Nearly every member of Colonel Lingo's force was on the bridge. King was about fifty feet from the officers when he brought the column to a halt. "We have a right to march," King answered. "This march will not continue," Cloud repeated. "It is not conducive to the safety of this group or to the motoring public." King then requested permission to pray. "You can have your prayer," Cloud said, "and then you must return to your church." After the singing of "We Shall Overcome" King then knelt and asked Rev. Ralph Abernathy to lead the demonstrators in prayer. "We come to present our bodies as a living sacrifice," Abernathy prayed. "We don't have much money, but we do have our bodies, and we lay them on the altar today." Afterwards, to most everyone's surprise, King rose and appeared to be turning the marchers around. As he did so, the troopers, in an unplanned move reportedly ordered over an open phone line from the governor's office in Montgomery, withdrew to the sides of the highway, leaving the highway open as if inviting the marchers to keep coming forward. But King did not take the bait, and instead turned the marchers around and led them back across the bridge.

The marchers were shocked, confused, and in disbelief. Many of them, especially those near the rear, had no idea what was going on up front, knowing only that they had come prepared to put their bodies on the line, but that now they were turning around. "All of a sudden I realized that the people in front were turning around and coming back," recalled Orloff Miller, a Unitarian minister from Boston. "I was aghast! What is going on? Are we not going through with this confrontation? What's happening?" Selma's teenagers and SNCC activists were especially angry. Jim Forman was livid. When he, and everyone else, learned that King had made an agreement with federal officials that morning to march only across the bridge, as a symbolic gesture, and then turn back, he exploded and denounced King for his "trickery." For Forman and many others in SNCC, this was the last straw. "SNCC had had enough," recalled John Lewis. "There would be no more working with the SCLC. There would be no waiting for any judge's injunction. SNCC was finished with waiting, finished with Selma." Many later remembered the ironic contradiction of marching *back* across the bridge all the while singing "Ain't gonna' let nobody turn me around." Jim Forman's frustration with what would come to be known as "Turnaround Tuesday" led him to rethink SNCC's involvement in the Selma campaign. Within twenty-four hours SNCC began to pull out of Selma and concentrate its activities in Montgomery.[6]

Back at Brown Chapel anger and frustration boiled over as King prepared to face his critics, who accused him of everything from duplicity to cowardice. Cleary aware that many movement activists felt betrayed, King explained that he had promised to proceed with the march only until violence was imminent. "We did march and we did reach the point of the brutality and we had a prayer service and a freedom rally. And we will go to Montgomery next week in numbers that no man can number." Feelings of frustration and betrayal notwithstanding, King aide Andrew Young gave perhaps the best assessment of King's decision to turn the marchers around. "The truth of it was there wasn't much else to do. We had been ordered by a judge not to go any further. If we had run into that police line, they would have beaten us up with court approval."[7] With SNCC having decided to pull out of Selma, King and SCLC searched for some kind of redemption. And, as sometimes happens, fate intervened.

After the humiliation of Turnaround Tuesday, King, realizing that many hundreds had traveled to Selma for that march, asked that as many of them as could remain in Selma for a few more days. More than four hundred clergymen, many of them white, had come to Selma in support of the voting rights campaign, and a good many of them responded to King's plea and decided to stay over. Among them were Reverends Orloff Miller, Clark Olsen, and James Reeb, all Unitarian ministers. Searching for a place to eat dinner on Tuesday evening—and having been warned that white restaurants would not take kindly to their presence—they found their way to a black-owned café, where they dined with other ministers, journalists, and movement activists. After their meal they left the diner and took a wrong turn that led them into hostile white territory. Having no idea of the danger they were in, they had accidentally walked past the Silver Moon Café, a restaurant so notoriously racist that it was the only white restaurant in Selma that movement activists had avoided "testing" after the passage of the 1964 Civil Rights Act. Suddenly, four or five white men from across the street started shouting at them, "Hey you niggers!" As Orloff Miller remembers, "We did not look across at them. We quickened our pace, we didn't run. We continued to walk in the same direction. And then they came across the street, from our left and from behind us. And one of them was carrying a club, and Clark said he turned around and saw the club, just as it was being swung. And Jim Reeb, being closest to the curb, caught the full impact of that blow." Reeb's attacker than yelled, "Here's how it feels to be a nigger down here!" The other men then kicked and punched Olsen and Miller, leaving all three ministers lying in the street.[8]

Miller and Olsen were finally able to get Reeb to his feet, but his injuries were serious. He was incoherent and disoriented and complaining of excruciating pain. At Amelia Boynton's insurance office, SNCC's Diane Nash quickly arranged for an ambulance to take Reeb and the others to Burwell Infirmary, a small black hospital that treated black and white movement activists. But Reeb's head injury was so severe that it was determined that he needed to be rushed to Birmingham University Hospital. Unfortunately, ten minutes into the trip, the ambulance blew a tire and eventually had to stop at a radio station to call for another. But just as Reeb was being transferred to the second ambulance, Dallas County deputies arrived and blocked the ambulance's exit. Whether intentional or not, the deputies' interrogation of the ministers caused precious time to be lost. When the deputies finally allowed the ambulance driver to proceed, they further demonstrated their lack of concern for Reeb's injuries by refusing to escort the ambulance to Birmingham. "You won't need an escort, and you don't need anybody to help," one of the deputies said to the group. Reaching a speed of 110 miles per hour at one point, the ambulance finally arrived at the hospital at around 11:00 p.m., nearly four hours after the assault. The doctors found that Reeb has sustained multiple skull fractures and quickly rushed him into surgery. The prognosis was grave.

Coming just two days after Bloody Sunday, this vicious attack on the thirty-eight-year-old white minister and father of four shocked the nation. Wednesday began with the nation's leading newspapers providing headline coverage to the preceding day's events, including sympathy marches that were held in Boston (Rev. Reeb's hometown), New York, Chicago, Los Angeles, Syracuse, Hartford, Detroit, and many other cities. On Capitol Hill, seven representatives and five senators delivered floor statements condemning the violence.

Back in Selma, a proposed march to the courthouse was blocked by Wilson Baker and Mayor Smitherman, but many of the marchers gathered for a prayer vigil at Brown Chapel. Meanwhile King, who for the most part had remained in seclusion following Tuesday's aborted march, prepared to leave for Montgomery where Judge Johnson's hearing would begin the next morning at 9:00 a.m.

On Thursday morning, March 11, King appeared in the Montgomery courtroom of Judge Frank Minis Johnson. Born in Haleyville, Alabama, in 1918, Frank Johnson was once referred to by journalist Bill Moyers as the judge who "some called the most hated man in the South, but a man who has earned an enduring place in our history for his courage and wisdom. His decisions changed the face of the South and helped to bring about a new American revolution."[9] During his twenty-four years on the federal bench as a judge for the United States District Court for the Middle District of Alabama (1955–1979), Johnson handed down a string of precedent-setting decisions that were met with staunch resistance in the white South but that ultimately helped reshape the nation's racial landscape. The youngest federal judge in the nation at the time of the 1956 Montgomery Bus Boycott that launched King's career as a civil rights leader, it was the thirty-eight-year-old Johnson who had cast the deciding vote striking down the Alabama law requiring segregated seating on buses. That decision, *Browder v. Gayle* (1956)—coming just two years after the Supreme Court's landmark ruling in *Brown v. Board of Education*—signaled that the federal judiciary was becoming more sympathetic to the demands of black civil rights activists, which consequently prompted movement leaders to turn increasingly to the courts for redress of grievances. Now, some nine years later at age forty-seven, Frank Johnson was a southern legend, revered by civil rights activists but hated by segregationists (Johnson's former friend and law school classmate Gov. George Wallace once referred to him as "a low-down, carpetbaggin', scalawaggin', race-mixin' liar"). While Johnson was not necessarily a civil rights advocate, he had a reputation for fairness and integrity, and on this Thursday morning, King was hoping that the judge would display both. While King's primary concern was whether the judge would grant an injunction preventing Alabama authorities from interfering with future marches, he nervously wondered whether he might be held in contempt for having led Tuesday's march, a clear violation of the judge's order.

Under questioning from the judge, King was forced to admit that LeRoy

Collins had brokered a deal whereby violence could be avoided if the march-ers simply turned around and did not confront the state troopers. Explaining to Judge Johnson that he never had any intention of marching to Montgom-ery, King said that he had feared what might happen if the march did not take place. "Thousands of people who had come to Selma to march were deeply aroused by the brutality of Sunday. I felt if I had not done it, pent-up emo-tions could have developed into an uncontrollable situation. I did it to give them an outlet." While King's explanation was sufficient to save him from a contempt citation, his candid admission of the brokered "deal" only increased the tensions between him and SNCC's leaders, some of whom had already told reporters privately that they felt as if King had betrayed the movement.[10]

Sometime later that evening, at around 8:00 p.m., Rev. James Reeb died in Birmingham Hospital. Presidential aide Marvin Watson informed President Johnson of the sad news, after which the president and first lady, Lady Bird Johnson, telephoned Reverend Reeb's widow and father to offer their condo-lences. Later, the president dispatched an Air Force C-140 jet to Birmingham to fly Mrs. Reeb and her father-in-law home to Boston. Across the nation thousands of people, especially white northerners, were visibly affected by the tragic death of the minister, and silent protests and demonstrations took place in scores of American cities, with many protestors carrying signs that read "We Mourn James Reeb." Many black activists, however, were angered that James Reeb's death had aroused the conscience of a nation that had largely been unmoved by the death of Jimmie Lee Jackson. President and Mrs. Johnson had telephoned their condolences to James Reeb's family, but no such expressions had been offered to the family of Jimmie Lee Jackson. "It seemed to me that the movement itself is playing into the hands of racism," SNCC activist Stokely Carmichael (later Kwame Touré) reflected. "Because what you want is a nation to be upset when *anybody* is killed, especially when one of *us* is killed, and so it's just playing into the hands of racism. And it's almost like, you know, in order for one of us to be recognized a white person must be killed—so what are you saying?"[11]

James Reeb's tragic death breathed new life into the stalled campaign in Selma. "Reverend Reeb now joins the ranks of those martyred heroes who have died in the struggle for freedom and human dignity," King said. He was "murdered by an atmosphere of inhumanity in Alabama that tolerated the vi-cious murder of Jimmie Lee Jackson . . . and the brutal beating of Sunday in Selma." Sheriff Jim Clark offered a very different assessment of both deaths.

According to Clark, Jackson "died under very mysterious circumstances," whereas Reeb died from injuries he received in a barroom fight. Although four men were arrested for the attack on Reeb, and three were indicted for murder, they were all later acquitted. In his eulogy on March 15 at Brown Chapel, King said that "James Reeb symbolizes the forces of good will in our nation. He demonstrated the conscience of the nation. He was an attorney for the defense of the innocent in the court of world opinion. He was a witness to the truth that men of different races and classes might live, eat, and work together as brothers."[12]

Tensions were running high in Selma. Demonstrations increased, and those who were holding an around-the-clock prayer vigil in a cold rain were pelted with rocks and bottles by unsympathetic whites. Four demonstrators were injured when snipers fired their rifles at the group. Meanwhile, in Washington, D.C., three thousand clergy from across the nation gathered to attend an interfaith rally called by the National Council of Churches' Commission on Religion and Race. On Friday morning, March 12, they filled a church on East Capitol Street to listen to reports of the brutality that many of their fellow clerics had witnessed in Selma, violence that had now claimed the life of one of their own. They then called on President Johnson to send a voting rights bill to Congress and provide protection for civil rights workers in Alabama. "I know that President Johnson is a deeply concerned and troubled man," said Methodist bishop John Wesley Lord, who had participated in the Turnaround Tuesday march. "But I also believe that due to the inability of the President to act . . . many Negroes and whites have become disenchanted and are in deep despair."[13]

The pressure on the president to act was mounting from all quarters. While the clergy were making their voices heard, a group of civil rights activists, led by Walter Fauntroy, the Washington, D.C., director of SCLC, met with the president for two hours in the Cabinet Room. Activists from SNCC, CORE, the Mississippi Freedom Democratic Party, as well as clergy, were also present. Angry activists demanded to know why the president had not yet sent a voting rights bill to Congress, as well as why he had not sent federal troops to Selma to protect the civil rights workers. The president explained that he wanted to send a bill to Congress that would pass, and not be filibustered. As for sending federal troops or marshals to Selma, Johnson urged caution, saying that he was reluctant to do anything that would drive white moderates into the staunchly segregationist camp. He did, however, inform the group that the Justice Department had filed an amicus brief supporting King's request that Judge Johnson prohibit Alabama authorities from interfering with another march. The president also stressed the importance of waiting for the judge's decision, and he also promised to send in troops if Governor Wallace refused to protect the marchers. As the meeting continued, more than one thousand demonstrators were protesting outside the White House, where they had been for several days. When Johnson joked that the demonstrators had been disturbing his family's sleep, a brash young SNCC activist named Hubert Brown quipped, "I don't think anyone is interested in whether your daughters could sleep or not. We are interested in the lives of our people."[14] Within a few years, Hubert Gerold Brown, better known as H. "Rap" Brown (now Jamil Abdullah Al-Amin) would gain national attention—and come under increasing scrutiny from state and federal authorities—for his fiery, revolutionary rhetoric. Elected chairman of SNCC in 1967 (replacing Stokely Carmichael), Brown would become one of the foremost advocates of "Black Power," and would eventually appear on the "FBI's Ten Most Wanted List" after avoiding trial on charges of inciting a riot and carrying a gun across state lines.

Immediately after his meeting with the civil rights activists, the president met with the delegation from the National Council of Churches. Included in this group was the Rev. Joseph Ellwanger, who had led sympathetic white Alabamians in their Saturday demonstration in Selma. As he had done with the first group, Johnson stressed his commitment to obtaining voting rights legislation, trying to convince the clergymen of his sincerity by recounting his previous achievements in civil rights. At one point in the meeting, Johnson likened himself to Abraham Lincoln, whose ghost, the president said, was "moving up and down the corridors of the [White House]." Although this meeting was more amicable than the previous one, many of the clerics left the meeting two hours later unconvinced of the president's sincerity, having heard the same promises many times before. When the president returned to his office later that afternoon, he learned that telegrams from all across the nation had been pouring into the White House demanding a voting rights bill.

And then, as the president had been expecting, he received a telegram from Governor Wallace requesting a meeting to discuss the situation in Selma. Johnson had been trying to reach Wallace for several days to arrange such a meeting, but most of the president's aides held out little hope that anything meaningful would result from it. They expected that Wallace, as he had done previously, would maintain his defiant posture, inevitably forcing the president's hand, much as Arkansas governor Orval Faubus had done with President Eisenhower in the school desegregation crisis at Central High School in Little Rock. Johnson, however, believed that Wallace might be more pliable, and that he was searching for some kind of exit strategy. President Johnson invited Governor Wallace to come to the White House the next day.

On Saturday morning, March 13, Governor Wallace flew into Washington, D.C., in the state's powder-blue airplane, which had a Confederate flag emblazoned on its side. After receiving a short briefing from Nicholas Katzenbach and Burke Marshall, Johnson invited Wallace and Seymore Trammel, Wallace's closest aide, into the Oval Office just before noon. What followed, as Katzenbach later recalled, was "the most amazing conversation I've ever been present at." The president directed the diminutive governor to take a seat on a couch, into which Wallace sank, further reducing his stature. Even though seated in his rocking chair, the six-foot-four-inch Johnson still towered over his southern guest. For the first few minutes it was all pleasant banter, but after introducing the governor to his two dogs, the president got down to business.

"Well, Governor, you wanted to see me?" Wallace began the conversation by blaming "malcontents, many of them trained in Moscow and New York," for causing trouble in the state. "You cannot deal with street revolutionaries," Wallace continued. "You can never satisfy them. First it is a front seat on the bus; next it's a takeover of the parks; then it's public schools; then it's voting rights; then it's jobs; then it's distribution of wealth without work." Johnson then looked at Wallace with a mixture of scorn and pity. "George, why are you doing this?" he asked. "You came into office a liberal—you spent all your life wanting to do things for the poor . . . Why are you off on this black thing? You ought to be down there calling for help for Aunt Susie in the nursing home." Trammel tried to interrupt the president, to shift the conversation back to what he and Wallace thought was the central issue—the Communist protestors who were tearing up Alabama—but Johnson refused to yield the floor.

"George," Johnson said, "do you see all of those demonstrators out in front of the White House?" "Oh yes, Mr. President, I saw them," Wallace replied. "Wouldn't it be just wonderful if we could put an end to all those demonstrations," Johnson asked. "Oh yes, Mr. President, that would be wonderful." Johnson then said, "Well, why don't you and I go out there, George . . . and let's announce that you've decided to [let the blacks vote] . . . in Alabama . . . Why don't you let the niggers vote? You agree they got the right to vote, don't you?" "Oh yes, there's no quarrel with that," Wallace said. "Well then, why don't you let them vote?" Johnson asked. "I don't have the power. That belongs to the county registrars in the state of Alabama," Wallace answered, to which Johnson replied, "George, don't you shit me as to who runs Alabama." Then, looking Wallace straight in the eye, Johnson said, "George, you're fucking over your president. Why are you fucking over your president? George, you and I shouldn't be thinking about 1964; we should be thinking about 1984. We'll both be dead and gone then." As Burke Marshall remembers, "Governor Wallace didn't quite grovel, but he was [very] pliant by the end of the two hours, with President Johnson putting his arm around him and squeezing him and telling him it's a moment of history, and how do we want to be remembered in history? Do we want to be remembered as petty little men, or do we want to be remembered as great figures that faced up to our moments of crisis?" The president had appealed to Wallace's better nature, and by now, as Marshall recalls, the governor "was like a rubber band." Johnson then escorted him out.[15]

While the president seemed emboldened and more determined after the two-hour exchange (actually more like a lecture with Johnson doing most of the talking), the meeting produced just the opposite effect on Wallace, causing one observer to comment that the governor had been reduced to "a mass of quivering flesh." Before leaving the White House Wallace met briefly with reporters, one of whom thought that he "looked considerably sobered and shorn of his accustomed cockiness." Ignoring the reporters' questions, Wallace thanked the president, who he called "a great gentleman, as always," for his hospitality. And then, flanked by Secret Service agents and police, he departed. Wallace later confessed to an aide that Johnson had simply overwhelmed him. "Hell," he said, "if I'd stayed in there much longer, he'd have had me coming out for civil rights."[16]

Later that afternoon Johnson met with more than one hundred reporters who had gathered in the Rose Garden for a special Saturday press conference. The light-hearted banter that usually preceded his press conferences was noticeably absent on this occasion, and the president appeared solemn. "What happened in Selma was an American tragedy," Johnson said. "The blows that were received, the blood that was shed, the life of the good man that was lost, must strengthen the determination of each of us to bring full equality and equal justice to all of our people. This is not just the policy of your government or your president. It is in the heart and the purpose and the meaning of America itself." The president then announced that he would send a bill to Congress to "strike down all restrictions used to deny the people the right to vote." It was the most forceful declaration ever made by an American president in support of equal voting rights.[17]

Later that evening the president and Mrs. Johnson attended a dinner party celebrating the appointment of a new American ambassador to Spain. "He was more in control of himself than I've ever seen," said one guest. "It was as if he had climbed a high place and could see things better than anyone else and fit them together." Another observer put it this way:

> He had heard the painful pleas from the blacks of Selma and Marion but had waited. He withstood the attacks brought on by Reverend Reeb's death and listened to angry clergymen and congressmen. But still he waited, allowing the pressure to build until public opinion polls indicated overwhelming support for a voting rights act. Now he could move forward, although the future remained far from clear. Not even Lyndon Johnson, master of Congress, could predict how the legislature would react on a subject so controversial as the place of black citizens in American life. But doing nothing was no longer a reasonable option. For Lyndon Johnson action was always the best medicine, better than exercise or sunshine. The chains that had bound him were broken, and the fog of depression that had plagued him had lifted.[18]

On Monday night, March 15, at 9:00 p.m. (EST), President Johnson addressed a joint session of Congress, the first time since 1946 that a sitting president had appeared before Congress to ask the body to consider a piece of legislation. Speaking before an estimated seventy million people who watched on television, President Johnson stood before Congress to announce his voting rights bill:

> I speak tonight for the dignity of man and the destiny of democracy. I urge every member of both parties—Americans of all religions and of all colors—from every section of this country—to join me in that cause. At times history and fate meet at a single time in a single place to shape a turning point in man's unending search for freedom. So it was at Lexington and Concord. So it was a century ago at Appomattox. So it was last week in Selma, Alabama. There is no Negro problem. There is no southern prob-

lem. There is no northern problem. There is only an American problem. And we are met here tonight as Americans—not as Democrats or Republicans—to solve that problem. . . . Many of the issues of civil rights are very complex and most difficult. But about this there can and should be no argument. Every American citizen must have an equal right to vote. There is no reason which can excuse the denial of that right. There is no duty which weighs more heavily on us than the duty we have to ensure that right. Yet the harsh fact is that in many places in this country, men and women are kept from voting simply because they are Negroes . . . Wednesday, I will send to Congress a law designed to eliminate illegal barriers to the right to vote. . . . This bill will strike down restrictions to voting in all elections, federal, state and local, which have been used to deny Negroes the right to vote. . . . What happened in Selma is part of a far larger movement which reaches into every section and State of America. It is the effort of American Negroes to secure for themselves the full blessings of American life. Their cause must be our cause too. Because it is not just Negroes, but really it is all of us, who must overcome the crippling legacy of bigotry and injustice. And we shall overcome . . .[19]

The initial reaction in the chamber to the president's very deliberate "And—we—shall—overcome" was stunned silence, as it gradually dawned on everyone present that Johnson had just publicly, in front of seventy million Americans, allied himself with the civil rights movement. But then the room erupted in applause, and most of the lawmakers stood on their feet. By evoking the movement's signature anthem, "We Shall Overcome," President Johnson had eliminated any lingering doubts about his commitment to the cause of racial equality, particularly at the ballot box. That symbolism was not lost on the southern congressmen, all of whom remained seated, withholding applause, stoic and resolute in their silent defiance. One cursed, "Goddamn." Other southern lawmakers had chosen another tack: no doubt fully apprised of the gist of the president's speech, the entire congressional delegations from Virginia and Mississippi, as well as some other southerners, had decided to boycott the event. While their absence hardly went unnoticed, it was the jubilant reaction of those present that gave the president the affirmation he sought. One presidential aide noted that "in the galleries, Negroes and whites . . . wept unabashedly."[20]

Back in Selma, the movement leaders had gathered in the home of Sullivan

Jackson to watch the president's speech on television. The Rev. C. T. Vivian remembers the moment well. "We were all sitting around together, and Martin was sitting in a chair looking toward the TV set, and when LBJ said, 'And we shall overcome,' we all cheered. And I looked over toward Martin, and Martin was very quietly sitting in the chair, and a tear ran down his cheek. It was a victory like none other. It was an affirmation of the movement." Selma's Mayor Smitherman had quite a different reaction to Johnson's speech. "Lyndon Johnson came on and said 'We shall overcome,' and it was just like you'd stuck a dagger in your heart, I mean, what's this guy doing? . . . it just destroyed everything we had allegedly been fighting for."[21]

Members of SCLC might have seen the president's speech as a victory of sorts, but SNCC's leaders did not. In Montgomery, SNCC's executive secretary James Forman remained skeptical, calling Johnson's use of the movement's phrase a "tinkling empty symbol" and said that the president had "spoiled a good song."[22] The day after the president's speech, Forman led a march in Montgomery to the capitol building; but the reception the protestors got suggested that the city police force was not quite ready to heed the president's call for an end to bigotry and injustice. Some of the activists were attacked by mounted city police who rode their horses into the crowd, and deputies used ropes, whips, and cattle prods to attack the demonstrators.

Speaking at a church rally later that night at Beulah Baptist Church, Forman said, "I want to know, did President Johnson mean what he said? See, that's what I want to know, because there's only one man in the country that can stop George Wallace and those posses. We can present thousands and thousands of bodies in the streets if we want to, and we can have all of the soul force and moral commitment around this world, but a lot of these problems will not be solved until [the man] in that shaggedy old place called the White House begins to shake and gets on the phone and says, 'Now listen, George, we're coming down there and throw you in jail if you don't stop that mess.' That's the only way it's going to be stopped. . . . I said it today, and I will say it again—if we can't sit at the table, let's knock the fuckin' legs off."[23] King rose to speak next, but the restless crowd, already fired up by Forman's speech (with a perfectly timed expletive thrown in for good measure) seemed unresponsive, an indication that SNCC's increasing militancy was gaining new converts, a development that worried King privately.

On Wednesday morning, March 17, King told a large crowd waiting for him in the rain that Montgomery city officials, worried about the violent turn of events, had agreed to exercise greater control over Sheriff Clark and his posse. While King was addressing the crowd through a bullhorn, an excited Andrew Young approached King and whispered something in his ear. When Young had finished, King returned to the bullhorn: "Let me give you this statement, which I think will come as an expression of deep joy to all of us. Judge Johnson has just ruled that we have a legal and constitutional right to march from Selma to Montgomery." The crowd erupted into applause. Standing beside King as he made the announcement, James Forman appeared not to share the euphoria of the moment. As they had done in the Bloody Sunday march, SNCC officials refused to endorse the demonstration, although they did allow SNCC members to participate individually. From the very beginning, SNCC's national chairman, John Lewis, was committed to the march; SNCC's executive secretary, James Forman, would eventually join the march as well.

Judge Johnson's ruling had cleared the way for the march to take place, but the question of who would protect the marchers on their five-day, fifty-four-mile journey from Selma to Montgomery remained. For his part, Governor Wallace made it clear at the outset that he opposed the march and had no intention of protecting it, saying that it would cause a financial burden on the state. "These people are pouring in from all over the country," an exasperated Wallace told President Johnson in a phone call on March 18. "It infuriates people . . . They're going to bankrupt the state." Knowing that the governor commanded ten thousand National Guardsmen, Johnson urged Wallace to call them up, but the governor refused. After getting off the phone with Wallace, the president remarked to an aide, "You're dealing with a very treacherous guy. He's a no good son of a bitch."[24]

With his popularity among white Alabamians at an all-time high, Wallace had little incentive to cooperate with the president. Wallace's fellow white citizens agreed with his characterization of the marchers as "Communist-trained anarchists" bent on disrupting Alabama's way of life. As he had done in 1963 when he stood in the doorway of the University of Alabama to block the entrance of two African American students, James Hood and Vivian Malone, George Wallace had once again thrown down the gauntlet, taking yet another symbolic stand in support of segregation. Addressing a special joint session of the state legislature, Wallace called Judge Frank Johnson "a hypocritical judge" who believed in "mob rule." He claimed that the march would bring to Alabama "every left wing, pro-Communist . . . and Communist in the country . . . along with the usual number of dupes and poor misguided individuals." The wild applause he received—some women wept—indicated that an overwhelming majority of the state's white residents shared his views.[25]

When it became clear that Wallace would not act to protect the marchers, President Johnson knew that he had to. The president federalized the Alabama National Guard, ordering 1,800 of its members to line the fifty-four mile route. Additionally, Johnson dispatched 2,000 army troops, 1,000 military policemen, 100 FBI agents, and another 100 federal marshals to assist in this military operation. Helicopters and light planes would patrol the route from the air, watching for snipers, and demolition teams would clear the way ahead, inspecting bridges and roadways for planted explosives. Deputy U.S. Attorney General Ramsey Clark supervised the effort, and Assistant Attorney General John Doar was assigned to accompany the marchers. With such an impressive display of military force, the president had clearly intended to make a strong political statement to both the marchers and to those who would oppose them. King had announced that the march would begin on Sunday, March 21. The marchers had five days to prepare.

John Lewis recalls that the next five days "were a swirl of activity, much like preparing an army for an assault." Marchers by the thousands from all across the nation were converging on Selma. A march of this size required detailed planning and organization, and issues such as food, communications, and security had to be addressed. The written records give some idea of the magnitude of this undertaking: "700 air mattresses, 700 blankets, four carnival-sized tents, 17,000 square feet of polyethylene for ground cloth, 700 rain ponchos, two 2,500-watt generators for campsite lighting, and 2,000 feet of electrical wiring."[26] Some of these items were donated, some were rented, and others were purchased, mainly with SCLC funds. Also needed were walkie-talkies, flashlights, pots and pans, and stoves for cooking. Ten local women cooked the evening meals in church kitchens in Selma, while ten others made sandwiches around the clock. Dozens of doctors and nurses from the same Medical Committee for Human Rights that had provided the medical assistance to those injured on Bloody Sunday were now on call again—this time with dozens of cases of rubbing alcohol and hundreds of boxes of Band-Aids for the marchers' sore muscles and blistered feet.

That Saturday night before the march, more than two hundred people gathered in Brown Chapel to prepare themselves spiritually for what lay ahead. James Bevel, Diane Nash, Andrew Young, John Lewis, along with a few others, made speeches to rally the troops. Well-known comedian and veteran movement activist Dick Gregory brought some levity to the occasion by joking, "It would be just our luck to find out that after all this Wallace is colored."[27]

The crowd that gathered at Brown Chapel on Sunday morning, March 21, was larger than King had hoped for. At around 12:30 in the afternoon he addressed the more than three thousand marchers who had assembled. "We are going to walk nonviolently and peacefully to let the nation and the world know we are tired now. We've lived with slavery and segregation 345 years, we've waited a long time for freedom. We are trying to remind the nation of the urgency of the moment. Now is the time to make real the promises of democracy; now is the time to transform Alabama, the heart of Dixie, to a state with a heart for brotherhood and peace and goodwill; now is the time to make justice a reality for all of God's children."[28]

And then the marchers began to move out, walking in a column that stretched over a mile long. Leading the way in the front row were Dr. King and his wife, Coretta, Ralph and Juanita Abernathy, A. Philip Randolph, Ralph Bunche, Andrew Young, Hosea Williams, John Lewis, James Forman, Dick Gregory, and Rabbi Abraham Heschel of the Jewish Theological Seminary of America. Assistant Attorney General for civil rights John Doar accompanied the marchers, presumably in an attempt to protect King from would-be assassins. Ahead of them was a television truck, with its lights and cameras capturing every historic step and, no doubt, providing King and the others some measure of protection. The march had drawn people from all over the country and from every walk of life. There was a one-legged man on crutches, Jim Letherer, from Saginaw, Michigan. When people thanked him for coming, he answered simply, "I believe in you. I believe in democracy." There was also Cager Lee, Jimmie Lee Jackson's elderly grandfather, who had been beaten the night his grandson was mortally wounded. Although the march exacted a heavy physical toll on him, he was determined to make the sacrifice, remarking that if Jimmie Lee "had to die for something, thank God it was for this."[29] There were also ministers, nuns, labor leaders, factory workers, schoolteachers, firemen, black, white, Native American, people from virtually every ethnic group.

As the marchers approached the Edmund Pettus Bridge, some briefly hesitated, perhaps reflecting privately on the nightmare they had endured on that very bridge exactly two weeks earlier. The same state troopers were there again. "This is the place where state troopers whipped us," Hosea Williams

After federal judge Frank M. Johnson lifted his injunction and ruled that the protesters had a constitutional right to demonstrate, more than three thousand marchers set out from Brown Chapel on March 21, 1965, exactly two weeks after Bloody Sunday, heading across the Edmund Pettus Bridge en route to Montgomery. This aerial view shows the marchers as they head out of Selma. Prints and Photographs Division, Library of Congress told King. "The savage beasts beat us on this ground." But on this occasion, the National Guard was present, and the marchers crossed over the bridge out of Selma without incident. At the foot of the bridge and at various other places along Jefferson Davis Highway the marchers faced a long line of hecklers, spewing streams of hateful venom. One white driver shouted, "Go to hell," while one of his children yelled, "Look at them niggers." Another white woman shouted at several nuns, "You're going to burn in hell with the rest of them." Whites held signs which read "I Hate Niggers," "Too Bad Reeb," and "Walk Coon." When a reporter asked Sheriff Clark if he had any feelings about the march, he remarked, "I'm glad to get rid of the ones that are leaving, but I wish they'd come back and get the rest of them."[30] Profanities and insults shouted from passing cars would be constant for most of the march, but the marchers seemed unaffected, maintaining their poise and dignity with every stride.

The marchers covered roughly seven miles the first day, and that night they rested at David and Rosa Bell Hall's 80-acre farm. The Halls lived with their eight children in a three-room shack without indoor plumbing. Neither of them was registered to vote. Fearing retaliation, the Halls had initially hesitated when approached about allowing the marchers to spend the night on their farm. But finally they agreed. When Mr. Hall was asked if he feared for his family's safety, he simply remarked, "The Lord will provide." When seventy-five-year-old Rosa Steele was asked the same question after she agreed to allow the marchers to spend the second night on her 240-acre farm in Lowndes County, she gave a similar response. "I'm not afraid. I've lived my three score and ten."[31]

The first night was cold, below freezing. More than two thousand of the marchers bedded down beneath three large tents—but first thing in the morning, most of them would have to return to Selma in a convoy of cars and buses. One of the conditions of Judge Johnson's order was that there could be no more than three hundred marchers on the second day, since this leg of the journey passed through a section of Lowndes County where the highway narrowed from four to two lanes. All of the marchers, however, made the most of that first evening together, building fires, clapping hands, and singing freedom songs until they finally fell asleep. For his part, King spent the first night in a sleeping bag inside a mobile van, the day's walking having left him with a painful blister on his left foot.

On Monday, day two of the march began uneventfully, though some of

The march from Selma to Montgomery covered fifty-four miles and took five days to complete. Walking through hostile territory and braving the elements, the marchers slept in makeshift tents set up along the highway. Pictured here is a procession of some of the marchers, accompanied by federal authorities who provided protection, and followed by trucks carrying equipment and supplies. Prints and Photographs Division, Library of Congress

the marchers were on edge after hearing rumors that local Klansmen had hidden bombs and land mines along the route. Well known for its long history of racist violence and the numerous blacks who had disappeared or died under mysterious circumstances there, "Bloody Lowndes" County had always been of particular concern to movement activists. There were also renewed attempts to discredit King as a leader, as the marchers came upon billboards depicting King as a Communist. Allegations of this sort were nothing new. FBI director J. Edgar Hoover had always maintained that King and the entire civil rights establishment were under Communist influence, accusations that had intensified in 1957 when King was photographed at the Highlander Folk School in Monteagle, Tennessee, a controversial center of progressive political activism (King had been invited to speak at the twenty-fifth anniversary of the school's founding). But King and the others ignored such distractions, focusing instead on the many blacks—those who were not part of the march—they encountered along the way. These black bystanders watched in awe as waves of marchers descended upon their communities. Occasionally, the marchers would stop briefly so that King could greet some of the local people who thought of him as a celebrity. "Are you people gonna' register to vote?" Andrew Young would ask. "We're not just marchin' here for fun." A good many responded with a resounding "Yes," most of whom later kept their promise.

The marchers covered sixteen miles on the second day, by now having walked a total of twenty-three miles. They sang many songs while they marched, but one of their favorites was

Pick 'em up and lay 'em down, right, right
Pick 'em up and lay 'em down, right, right,
Oh the mud sure was deep, right, right,
I got blisters on my feet, right, right,
Pick 'em up and lay 'em down, right, right,
All the way to Selma town, right, right.

They all needed rest badly, and some of them, like King, required medical attention for blistered feet and sunburn. On Tuesday, day three, the weather was absolutely miserable, but still the marchers managed to cover eleven miles. A hard, cold rain fell all day, and everyone was drenched. The marchers had to improvise quickly, turning cereal boxes into hats and sheets of plastic into ponchos. John Lewis remembers that "No one complained; no one got tired; no one fell back." King had walked most of the miles on the first three days, but badly blistered feet forced him to take a break after Tuesday. King rested Wednesday morning as the others set out for a sixteen-mile walk that would bring them to the western outskirts of Montgomery. At midday, King left the group briefly to travel to Cleveland to speak at a fundraising event that had been arranged earlier, but planned to return to Alabama late that night for Thursday's final march into Montgomery.[32]

Many would describe Wednesday night, the last night of the march, as an unforgettable experience. Arriving on the outskirts of Montgomery at the end of their fourth day, the marchers were sunburned, blistered, weather-beaten, and, as one reporter described, looking like the "last stragglers of a lost battalion." Their final stop was on the grounds of a place called the City of St. Jude, a Catholic medical, religious, and educational complex, and the site of the first integrated hospital in the southeastern United States. King had

Rev. Dr. Martin Luther King, Jr., president of SCLC and undisputed leader of the civil rights movement, had come to Selma in January 1965 at the request of Amelia Boynton, Selma's leading black activist. Here, King is pictured marching with his chief SCLC lieutenant, Rev. Ralph D. Abernathy (reading the newspaper). Prints and Photographs Division, Library of Congress returned to the march by this time, and at the request of singer/actor Harry Belafonte, dozens of celebrities joined the marchers for a massive outdoor concert. The list of stars was virtually a "Who's Who" of the entertainment world. Among them were Tony Bennett, Sammy Davis, Jr., Billy Eckstine, Shelley Winters, Ossie Davis, Leonard Bernstein, Mahalia Jackson, Nina Simone, Odetta, Johnny Mathis, Nipsey Russell, Peter, Paul, and Mary, the Chad Mitchell Trio, Anthony Perkins, Elaine May, George Kirby, Joan Baez, Dick Gregory, and others. They all performed that evening on a makeshift stage fashioned from stacks of coffins loaned by a local black funeral home. More than 20,000 people gathered for hours of songs and speeches in what would come to be known as the "Stars for Freedom" concert. When a reporter asked Elaine May if she thought this show and all the celebrities were turning a serious march into a circus, she shot back, "The only real circus is the state of Alabama and George Wallace."[33]

On Thursday morning, March 25, the final day of the march, the beautiful sunny weather seemed to signal a promising forecast for the day, until dark clouds of another nature arose. Assistant Attorney General John Doar informed Andrew Young that he had received reports that a sniper was planning to assassinate King as the marchers entered Montgomery. Doar explained that the FBI was doing what it could to guarantee King's safety, but there simply was not enough time to check every possible location for a would-be assassin. Doar strongly advised King to leave the march and arrive in Montgomery by car, but King refused, insisting "I have to march and I have to be in the front line." Knowing that it would futile to try to persuade King otherwise, Young devised a strategy that he hoped would save his leader's life. "Martin always wore the good preacher blue suit. And I figured that since we couldn't stop him from marching, we just had to believe it was true when white folks say we all look alike. So everybody that was about Martin's size and had on a blue suit, I put in the front of the line with him. . . . Now there were some very important people who felt as though they were being pushed back, but all of the preachers loved the chance to get up in the front line with Martin Luther King. But I don't think to this day most of them know why they were up there."[34]

And then the marchers, now numbering roughly 30,000, made their way through downtown Montgomery, around the fountain on Court Square, up Dexter Avenue past the church where King had pastored for six years, finally reaching the silver and white state capitol building, where the Alabama state

After five days on the road, the marchers were finally on the outskirts of Montgomery. Despite confirmed threats against his life, Dr. King refused to leave the march and insisted on being with the marchers as they entered Montgomery. King is pictured here, being flanked by other movement leaders, with James Forman of SNCC to his immediate left. Andrew Young, SCLC's executive secretary, is in front. Prints and Photographs Division, Library of Congress flag flew high above the rotunda dome, along with the flag of the Confederacy. John Lewis observed that "the American flag was nowhere in sight." Neither was Governor Wallace, though he occasionally peeked through his office blinds.

A podium had been set up on the trailer of a flatbed truck, along with a microphone and loudspeakers. Peter, Paul, and Mary sang, followed by the speakers, including Ralph Bunche, Roy Wilkins, James Farmer, Whitney Young, Rosa Parks, Ralph Abernathy, Fred Shuttlesworth, James Bevel, Bayard Rustin, and John Lewis. Amelia Boynton read a petition the marchers hoped to present to the governor at the conclusion of the day's events, and Albert Turner, leader of the Marion, Alabama, contingent and friend to the martyred Jimmie Lee Jackson, drew laughs when he told the crowd, "I look worse than anybody else on this stage. That's because I marched fifty miles." The preliminaries had been necessary, but it was now approaching 4:00 in the afternoon, and the restless thousands longed to hear from Martin Luther King himself.

King finally stepped to the podium, delivering one of his most powerful speeches. Though not as well remembered as some of his other orations, many believe that his speech on this occasion rivaled his "I Have a Dream" speech, delivered at the March on Washington on August 28, 1963, and his "Mountaintop" speech, delivered in Memphis, Tennessee, on April 3, 1968, that eerily foretold of his assassination the very next day. "Last Sunday, more than eight thousand of us started on a mighty walk from Selma, Alabama. We have walked on the meandering highways and rested our bodies on rocky byways . . . Sister Pollard . . . who lived in this community during the [bus] boycott . . . was asked if she wanted a ride, and when she answered 'no,' the person said, 'Well, aren't you tired?' And with ungrammatical profundity she said, 'My feets is tired, but my soul is rested.'" Looking out over the massive crowd, with the Alabama state capitol and the Confederate flag in the background, King said "They told us we wouldn't get here. And then there were those who said that we would get here only over their dead bodies. But all the world today knows that we *are* here and we are standing before the forces of power in the state of Alabama, saying 'We ain't gonna let nobody turn us around.' We are on the move now and no wave of racism can stop us." King continued:

> We must come to see that the end we seek is a society at peace with itself, a society that can live with its conscience. That will be a day not of the white

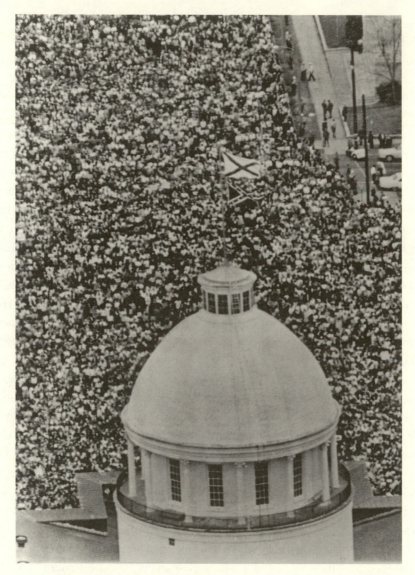

A sea of demonstrators numbering 30,000 arrives at Montgomery on Thursday, March 25, their journey complete. Alabama's state flag and the Confederate battle flag can be seen flying atop the state capitol. Moments later, Martin Luther King would deliver one of his most famous speeches, saying that "We must come to see that the end we seek is a society at peace with itself, a society that can live with its conscience. That will be a day not of the white man, not of the black man. That will be the day of man as man." Prints and Photographs Division, Library of Congress man, not of the black man. That will be the day of man as man. I know some of you are asking today, "How long will it take?" I come to say to you this afternoon that however difficult the moment, however frustrating the hour, it will not be long; because truth crushed to earth will rise again. How long? Not long, because no lie can live forever. How long? Not long, because you will reap what you sow. How long? Not long, because the arc of the moral universe is long, but it bends toward justice. How long? Not long, because mine eyes have seen the glory of the coming of the Lord, He's trampling out the vintage where the grapes of wrath are stored. He has loosed the faithful lightning of His terrible swift sword. His truth is marching on. Glory hallelujah! *Glory Hallelujah! Glory hallelujah! Glory hallelujah!* His truth is marching on.[35]

The jubilant crowd that had been hanging on King's every word, punctuating every phrase with "Preach, doctor," now erupted, cheering and clapping so loudly that the sound reverberated throughout the city. Then they sang "We Shall Overcome," a fitting conclusion for such a momentous occasion. Meanwhile, nervous Justice Department officials, fearful of an attempt on King's life, looked on with a sense of relief as the day's events came to an end. But the day was not yet over for Amelia Boynton and the delegation appointed to present Governor Wallace with their list of grievances. When they marched to the capitol steps, state troopers blocked them, informing them that the governor was no longer in his office. When they tried to get through a few minutes later they managed to see the governor's secretary, but he refused to commit the governor to any future meeting. By all appearances, the "day of man as man" that King spoke of had not yet arrived in Montgomery.

Martin Luther King's majestic oratory provided a triumphant conclusion to the Selma to Montgomery march, but the hardest work still lay ahead. Although initially slow to act—and perhaps believing that he had already fulfilled his promise to honor the memory of the late President Kennedy by securing passage of the 1964 Civil Rights Act—President Johnson had been deeply affected by the events of those previous two weeks, so much so that he had embraced both the language and the spirit of the movement. But convincing southern whites and their elected congressional representatives to open up the ballot box to the descendants of former slaves would be no easy walk. As the protestors would soon discover, there would be one last stand yet to be made in the heart of Dixie.

5

A Season of Suffering

All my life I believed that white power could and would draw the line whenever and wherever it wanted, and there was absolutely nothing black people could do about it. The civil rights movement would force some concessions. But there was a limit to how much accommodation the white South would make . . .

—J. L. Chestnut, Jr., a black attorney and Selma resident

THE FIVE-DAY, FIFTY-FOUR-MILE MARCH from Selma to Montgomery was over, and everyone from Justice Department officials to the marchers themselves could finally breathe a sigh of relief. Violence along the way had always been a real possibility, and any rumors of an assassination attempt against Dr. King had been taken seriously. No one expressed a greater sense of relief that the march had been pulled off without violence than Andrew Young. After returning to Dexter Avenue Baptist Church, Young "just let the tears flow," he later recalled. "Tears of relief that we had completed the march without any bloodshed, that we had actually pulled it off . . . a feat we could not possibly have foreseen when we were beginning our campaign."[1]

The march itself was over, but now came the challenge, both figuratively and literally, of getting the marchers out of town before sundown. The marchers had been advised to leave Montgomery as quickly as possible; as the National Guard and the federal troops gradually withdrew, the likelihood of some kind of confrontation increased. Some of the marchers boarded trains and planes as they prepared to head home, while others, mainly those who were local, relied on various types of ground transportation in order to reach their destinations. SCLC's James Orange, who was in charge of local transportation, urged the marchers to use the movement's vehicles and travel in a caravan for added safety, rather than drive their own cars, which would leave them more isolated and vulnerable. Further, any cars having out-of-state license plates could easily be singled out and would become likely targets for local whites itching to start trouble. As an added measure of protection, white volunteers were advised that as much as possible, they should avoid being seen in the company of blacks, a message that SNCC especially had been preaching to white northern volunteers before and since the murders of Chaney, Goodman, and Schwerner several months earlier during Mississippi Summer.

Whites from all across the country had converged on Selma for the march. One of them was Viola Gregg Liuzzo, a thirty-nine-year-old homemaker and mother of five from Detroit, Michigan. A Unitarian Universalist with a history of civil rights activism in Detroit who had joined the NAACP in 1964, Liuzzo had answered King's call for people of goodwill to come to Selma to help focus the nation's attention on racial injustice. During her stay in Selma she had lived with a black family in public housing, caring for her hosts' grandchildren and assisting the medical team at St. Jude. She had participated in the Selma to Montgomery march, sleeping in her car and helping out with coordination and logistics wherever she was needed.[2]

On the evening of March 25, as people began volunteering to drive the marchers back to Selma, Liuzzo once again offered her services. But James Orange, the veteran SCLC activist who had nearly been lynched in a Marion jail a month earlier and was well aware of the danger, advised against it. "Vi, don't go out there," Orange recalled telling her. "We've got trucks, we've got busses; there's no reason for you to use your car on that highway."[3] Apparently unaware of the real danger she faced, Liuzzo insisted on doing her part and decided to add her car to the transportation pool. After dropping off one group of marchers at Brown Chapel, she headed back toward Montgomery, accompanied by nineteen-year-old Leroy Moton, a black SCLC volunteer who had carried an American flag during the march. When the interracial pair stopped for gas at a filling station, they were subjected to a barrage of racist insults.

Liuzzo's Oldsmobile with Michigan license plates made an easy target for the four Ku Klux Klansmen who followed her on Route 80 through Lowndes County. After bumping her car from the rear, the Klansmen pulled their car alongside hers. One of the men inside the car opened fire, spraying the car with bullets. Two of the bullets struck Liuzzo in the head, killing her instantly, causing her car to run into a ditch. Miraculously, despite being covered with blood, Moton had not been hit. When the Klansmen returned to the crime scene to check on their victims, Moton remained motionless, pretending to be dead. Moton remembered hearing one Klansman say to another, "Are you sure he's dead?" The other one answered, "When I plug a nigger, I plug him good. He's dead." Once the Klansmen drove off, Moton began searching for help, eventually flagging down a truck driven by Rev. Leon Riley, who was also shuttling marchers back to Selma.

Because he had to play dead in order to save his own life, Moton could offer few details about the murderers. But within hours, the FBI learned that one of its undercover informants had been in the car with the Klansmen. That next day, President Johnson went on national television to announce that Mrs. Liuzzo's killers had been identified and were in custody, all four of them members of the Alabama Ku Klux Klan. "Mrs. Liuzzo went to Alabama to serve the struggle for justice," the president said. "She was murdered by the enemies of justice who, for decades, have used the rope and the gun, the tar and the feathers, to terrorize their neighbors. They struck by night, as they generally do, for their purpose cannot stand the light of day."[4] Appearing on the *Today* show, Governor Wallace was far less sympathetic. "Of course I regret the incident, but I would like to point out that people are assaulted in every state in the union . . . And with 25,000 marching in streets and chanting and maligning and slandering and libeling the people of this state, as they did for several hours on this network and the other networks, I think the people of our state were greatly restrained."[5]

It was clear to all observers that President Johnson had taken an unusual interest in Viola Liuzzo's murder, perhaps because, as some speculated, she was a white woman—the only white woman to be killed in the civil rights movement. The president announced that he had empowered the attorney general to create new legislation to combat the Klan and that he had also encouraged Congress to investigate the Klan and other violent organizations as well. Liuzzo's murder was a brutal reminder, as one observer put it, "that the true reality of Alabama was not King's melodious phrases but racist violence delivered without warning." It also served as a chilling affirmation that King had been right when he predicted that a "season of suffering" still lay ahead.[6]

President Johnson's statement that all of the Klansmen implicated in Mrs. Liuzzo's murder were in custody was not entirely true. One of the accused, thirty-four-year-old Gary Thomas Rowe, was not in jail but instead was helping the FBI build a solid case against his accomplices. Rowe, it turns out, had been the FBI's top informant inside the Alabama Klan for the previous five years. Rowe insisted that fellow Klansman Collie Leroy Wilkins had fired the fatal shots that killed Liuzzo. Although Rowe admitted to having stuck his gun out of the car window pretending to shoot, he claimed not to have fired a single shot. For whatever reason, the FBI never tested Rowe's gun or the bullet casings for fingerprints, causing many to speculate that Rowe may have been more involved in the murder than he admitted.

There was good reason for that speculation. Although an informant for the FBI since 1960, Rowe's involvement with the Alabama Klan had been brutal and bloody, which he insisted had been necessary in order to establish his racist bona fides. He had organized and participated in the attack on the Freedom Riders in Birmingham in May of 1961, and may have played some role in the bombing of the Sixteenth Street Baptist Church in Birmingham in September 1963 that resulted in the murders of four black girls. Fueling the speculation even more, it was soon revealed that on the day of Liuzzo's murder (before the shooting) Rowe had actually called his FBI contact to notify the bureau that Klansmen were traveling to Montgomery and that violence was planned. Once the press became aware of this, and began to ask why Rowe had not tried to prevent the murder, FBI director J. Edgar Hoover began a cover-up campaign to ensure that the FBI would not be implicated in Liuzzo's murder by allowing an informant to engage in criminal activities.[7]

To divert attention from Rowe, Hoover initiated a smear campaign to discredit Mrs. Liuzzo in the eyes of the public. In taped conversations with President Johnson, Hoover insinuated that it was not Liuzzo's righteous indignation against racism that had brought her south, but rather her wanton lust for black men. And, at least according to Hoover, she was also a drug addict. Hoover told the president that Liuzzo's body had exhibited "numerous needle points indicating that she may have been taking dope," and that the Klansmen had likely targeted her because they saw "this colored man . . . snuggling up pretty close to the white woman . . . it had all the appearances of a necking party."[8] The FBI also leaked the lurid allegations to the media, and several newspapers repeated the claims, none of which was true. Autopsy results showed no traces of any drugs in Liuzzo's body at the time of her death, nor was there any indication of recent sexual activity. The FBI's role in the smear campaign against Viola Liuzzo was not uncovered until thirteen years after her murder, when her children obtained case documents from the FBI under the Freedom of Information Act.

The lies and distortions that Hoover had disseminated regarding Mrs. Liuzzo would become exhibit one for the defense during the trial of the three men accused of her murder. The jury was seated on May 3, and the defendants were Collie Wilkins, age twenty-one and the alleged trigger man, William Eaton, forty-one, and Eugene Thomas, forty-two. FBI informant Gary Rowe was not indicted and served as a witness for the prosecution. Defending the three was Matthew Hobson Murphy, who held the position of Klan Imperial Klonsul (chief legal counsel). In an overt attempt to influence the all-white jury, Murphy referred to Liuzzo as a "nigger lover" lusting after "black meat." This blatant appeal to racism resonated with at least two of the jurors, who refused to vote for a conviction, causing a mistrial. But before the re-trial got underway, defense attorney Murphy fell asleep at the wheel on August 20 and was killed when his car collided with a gasoline truck. Birmingham's former mayor and staunch segregationist Art Hanes agreed to take over as defense counsel. The re-trial began on October 20, and this time another all-white jury took less than two hours to acquit the defendants. But in a federal courtroom in December 1965, with Judge Frank M. Johnson presiding and Assistant Attorney General John Doar prosecuting, the defendants were convicted of violating Viola Liuzzo's civil rights, and each was sentenced to ten years in prison. Rowe was the prosecution's star witness, and in recognition of his services, the FBI gave him a $10,000 reward and a new identity. When Rowe died of a heart attack in Savannah, Georgia, in May 1998, he was buried under the name Thomas Neal Moore. His obituary was not published until that October.

On Tuesday, March 30, Viola Liuzzo's funeral was held at the Immaculate Heart of Mary Catholic Church in Detroit. Among the many dignitaries present were Dr. King, Roy Wilkins of the NAACP, James Farmer of CORE, Michigan lieutenant governor William G. Milliken, United Auto Workers president Walter Reuther, and Teamsters president Jimmy Hoffa. Both Dr. King and Vice President Hubert Humphrey visited the family to pay their respects.

Mrs. Liuzzo was laid to rest at the Holy Sepulcher Cemetery in Southfield, Michigan. One week later, a charred cross was found at the Liuzzo residence.

Calculated acts of violence and brutality, especially the murders of a white clergyman and a white homemaker with five children, could prove useful to a nonviolent movement, and the escalating terror gave momentum to those who had been pushing for a voting rights bill. But getting additional civil rights legislation through Congress, even with the president's support, was by no means certain. When the Civil Rights Act finally went to the Senate in the spring of 1964, southern lawmakers succeeded in delaying passage by mounting the longest filibuster in American history. These forces of obstruction could be counted on to resist any new voting legislation with equal vigor and determination.

King intended to keep up the pressure. He had been terribly despondent in the aftermath of the Selma march, not only because of Viola Liuzzo's murder, but also because he had seen no tangible improvements in the lives of Alabama's black residents. King stressed that the Alabama campaign was not intended to end with the march, but that SCLC would continue to engage in voter registration efforts throughout the state. He also spoke in favor of a nationwide boycott of all of Alabama's products, hoping that economic pressure might yield positive results where moral suasion had failed. He also hoped to ease the tensions that now existed between SCLC and SNCC and helped to arrange a series of meetings between the two organizations, with Harry Belafonte acting as intermediary, aimed at better coordinating their voting registration efforts.

Meanwhile on Capitol Hill, there were renewed discussions about a voting rights bill. The bill's sponsors in the Senate, Democrat leader Mike Mansfield and Republican leader Everett Dirksen, presented a bill to the body on March 17. The bill had sixty-four Senate sponsors, an indication that there was bipartisan support—something that would be necessary in order to prevent a southern filibuster. But the first legislative steps were always the most difficult, because the bill had to go to the Senate Judiciary Committee, which as one observer put it, was "traditionally the graveyard of civil rights legislation." Chairing that powerful committee was Mississippi's James Eastland, a twenty-year veteran of the Senate and owner of one of the largest plantations in Sunflower County, where only 161 blacks out of a population of 13,524 were registered to vote. A virulent racist, Eastland had vehemently opposed the Supreme Court's *Brown v. Board of Education* school desegregation decision, expressing his defiance by proudly proclaiming, "Supreme Court or no Supreme Court, we intend to maintain segregated schools down here in Dixie." Reveling in his power to tie up any civil rights legislation that came to his committee, he was anything but ambivalent in expressing his views on the proposed voting rights legislation: "Let me make myself clear. I am opposed to every word and every line in it."[9]

Senator Eastland would be joined by most of his usual allies—composing what was often referred to as the "southern bloc"—in their concerted effort to defeat the bill. Georgia's Senator Herman Talmadge said the bill was "grossly unjust and vindictive in nature," while South Carolina's Strom Thurmond predicted that America would become a "totalitarian state" if the bill passed. Louisiana's Allen Ellender planned "to talk against it as long as God gives me breath."[10] But the southern demagogues suffered a major defeat when Majority Leader Mansfield's motion holding the committee to a strict deadline by which to complete its work (thereby frustrating their stalling tactics) passed by a large margin.

For many years, the powerful southern bloc had successfully resisted or delayed key civil rights legislation, but by 1965 cracks were beginning to appear in their armor. Many of the older and more powerful veterans were either in poor health, suffering from battle fatigue, or beginning to grudgingly accept the fact that African Americans could no longer be excluded from the political process. Georgia's Richard B. Russell, for many years the undisputed leader of the southern bloc who had devoted his entire career to opposing civil rights legislation, was now suffering from emphysema and a pulmonary edema and seemed resigned to the bill's passage. "If there is anything I could do, I would do it," he told a friend, "but I assume the die is cast." Virginia's Harry Byrd and Willis Robertson, both in their late seventies, seemed to share his sentiments, with Byrd telling an aide, "You know, you can't stop this bill. We can't deny the Negroes a basic constitutional right to vote." South Carolina's Olin Johnston, an ardent segregationist who as governor had allowed the execution of the youngest person in the United States in the twentieth century—a fourteen-year-old black boy whose conviction of murdering two white girls has been referred to as "suspicious at best and a miscarriage of justice at worst"—died of cancer on April 18. Other members of the southern bloc gradually broke ranks, some on moral grounds, and others because of the new reality that at some point in the not too distant future they would have to pay a heavy political price at the hands of a newly empowered black electorate.[11]

For the next few weeks the bill moved from subcommittee to committee in both the House and the Senate, undergoing changes and revisions. As southern conservative influence had declined, northern liberal influence had increased, and younger senators like Indiana's Birch Bayh, Maryland's Joseph Tydings, and Massachusetts's Edward Kennedy were being joined by the liberal veterans, such as New York's Jacob Javits. The bill was getting support from Democrats and Republicans, North and South. As further evidence of the bipartisan support the bill enjoyed, on April 8, a coalition of nine Democrats and Republicans added five provisions to the new draft of the bill to make it stronger. These changes included the suspension of literacy tests in twenty-six states, including Alabama, Georgia, and Mississippi, the three states that had been the focus of so many civil rights campaigns; the requirement that federal examiners automatically be dispatched to any covered jurisdiction where less than 25 percent of the minority voting-age population was registered (an indication that patterns of abuse were continuing); a provision calling for Civil Service Commission poll watchers at future elections; and a provision that increased the criminal penalties for attempting to prevent from voting those who had been registered.

Although weakened and somewhat dispirited, the southern bloc was not about to go down without one last fight. With Louisiana's Allen Ellender and North Carolina's Sam Ervin leading the charge, the southern forces continued to offer up amendments aimed at weakening the bill, and failing that, they resorted to their old technique of talking the bill to death by filibuster. The only way to defeat a filibuster was by invoking cloture, a parliamentary procedure in the Senate designed to end debate and force an up or down vote on the bill. Two-thirds of the Senate had to vote for cloture, and achieving the necessary votes would require a bipartisan effort. On May 22 the Senate leadership filed a cloture petition to end debate, and the final vote was scheduled for May 25. All one hundred of the senators were present in the chamber for the vote, and when the votes were counted, seventy voted in favor of cloture—forty-seven Democrats and twenty-three Republicans. Twenty-one Democrats and nine Republicans voted against. The cloture motion had passed with a margin of three votes more than the sixty-seven required. The handwriting appeared to be on the wall, and a final vote on the bill was scheduled for the next day.

On May 26, ten weeks after President Johnson had submitted the bill to Congress, the final vote on the voting rights bill was taken in the Senate. The bill passed by a margin of 77–19 (forty-seven Democrats and thirty Republicans voting in favor, seventeen Democrats and two Republicans voting against). All of the Democrats voting against the bill were from the South, and the two Republican opponents were South Carolina's Strom Thurmond and Texas's John Tower. In anticipation of the bill's passage, state lawmakers in both Alabama and Mississippi were engaging in futile efforts to alter their state laws so that their states might escape coverage by the provisions of the soon-to-be-enacted voting rights bill.

The voting rights bill had cleared its first major hurdle, but now it was headed to the House of Representatives. The president's party held a 295–140 majority in the House, but many of those Democrats hailed from southern states and Johnson knew there would be opposition. The bill's eventual passage was expected, but the House would surely debate its own version of the bill, and if substituted amendments produced lengthy delays anything could happen. If the House version of the bill differed significantly from the Senate version, then the process would have to begin all over again, and with the likelihood of a southern filibuster still looming, the bill's supporters had good reason to be concerned.

The House Judiciary Subcommittee considered the bill for twelve days and heard from fifty-six witnesses before sending the bill to the full Judiciary Committee, chaired by New York's Democratic congressman Emanuel Celler. The House version would differ from the Senate version in a couple of significant ways. The Senate version had penalized *officials* (but not private citizens) who tried to prevent blacks from voting, but the House version changed that to apply to *anyone* who threatened or injured those encouraging blacks to vote. And, unlike the Senate bill, the House added a provision banning all poll taxes. But when the full committee issued its report on June 1, it was clear that there were some divisions within the committee. Congressman William McCulloch of Ohio, the ranking Republican on the Judiciary Committee, wanted to eliminate both the poll tax ban as well as the automatic trigger that suspended literacy tests in those places (mainly southern states) that required them and where less than 50 percent of the citizens had voted in the last presidential election. He, along with Michigan Republican and House Minority Leader Gerald Ford, cosponsored a new bill, HR 7896, to be debated by the full House.

The bill was then sent to the Rules Committee, controlled by ardent segregationist Howard Smith of Virginia. Well known for his opposition to civil rights legislation, Smith referred to the bill as "venomous" and "abominable"[12] and, as expected, delayed holding hearings until criticism forced him to begin the process on June 24. House debate on the administration's version began on July 6 and immediately faced a challenge from the backers of the Ford-McCulloch bill. McCulloch's bill removed the ban on the poll tax and the automatic trigger that punished southern states primarily. In his version, once the attorney general received twenty-five legitimate complaints of voter intimidation, he would be empowered to send federal registrars to investigate. Potential voters would not have to take a literacy test if they could produce evidence of a sixth-grade education. If not, they had to demonstrate literacy to a federal registrar. In other words, literacy tests would not be *automatically* eliminated in states with poor voter turnout, nor were southern states with the worst voting records *automatically* required to submit new voting laws to Washington. White House spokesmen, joined by King and other civil rights advocates, argued that the automatic trigger was necessary, believing (and with good reason) that blacks having to take the initiative to seek redress of grievances would be intimidated and harassed by the same state and local officials who had opposed blacks voting in the first place.

But just when it appeared that momentum was building for the Ford-McCulloch version, Virginia congressman William Tuck, a vocal segregationist and former governor, unintentionally sealed the bill's fate by attaching to it the racist stigma that the bill's supporters had deftly tried to avoid. Apparently unaware of the negative impact that his candid remarks would have on his House colleagues, Tuck said that voting for the original bill supported by the president would "foist upon your constituents this unconstitutional monstrosity" that would guarantee that blacks would vote, and that he hoped "that every member *opposed* to these so-called voting rights bills would vote *for*" the Ford-McCulloch substitute bill (emphasis added).Tuck's comments proved to be a terrible blunder. Minority Leader Gerald Ford tried to repair the damage, but many Republicans who had been leaning in support of the substitute bill now quickly abandoned it.[13]

On July 9, the House of Representatives passed the voting rights bill by a vote of 333–85. Among the majority were 112 Republicans (3 from the South) and 33 southern Democrats, including Majority Whip Hale Boggs of Louisiana, who shortly before the final vote found himself at odds with his friend and Louisiana colleague Joe D. Waggoner. A conservative Democrat, Waggoner had spoken against the bill, claiming that blacks in Louisiana could vote as freely as anyone else. Although Boggs had intended to vote for the bill, he had not planned to speak in support of it—that is, until he listened to Waggoner's oration. After Waggoner had finished speaking, Boggs rose to offer a decidedly different perspective: "I wish I could stand here as a man who loves his state, born and reared in the South . . . and say there has not been discrimination . . . but unfortunately it is not so. . . . I shall support this bill because I believe the fundamental right to vote must be a part of this great experiment in human progress under freedom which America is." The chamber erupted in applause, and Boggs received a standing ovation.[14]

Because the House bill contained the poll tax ban which the Senate had rejected, the bill would go to a joint House–Senate Conference Committee whose members would try to settle the differences. When their first meeting in late July yielded no results, Attorney General Katzenbach drafted a new provision that, while not banning the poll tax outright, contained much stronger language regarding the tax. While some on the committee felt that the new language was a compromise they could live with, some of the more liberal members felt that the provision did not go far enough. At this point, an exasperated President Johnson and Katzenbach turned to Dr. King, hoping that he might be able to break the impasse. Though disappointed that the Senate bill did not ban the poll tax, King certainly did not want this single issue to derail the bill. In an attempt to break the logjam, Katzenbach assured King that the administration would assert explicitly that the poll tax was unconstitutional and that the Justice Department would sue those states that still maintained it. King agreed to the compromise, and then issued a statement to that effect. "While I would have preferred that the bill eliminate the poll tax . . . once and for all," King's statement read, "it does contain an express declaration by Congress that the poll tax abridges and denies the right to vote. . . . I am confident that the poll tax provision of the bill—with vigorous action by the Attorney General—will operate finally to bury this iniquitous device."[15]

King's public endorsement of the compromise was enough to satisfy the more liberal members of the House–Senate Conference Committee, and on July 29 they agreed to remove the poll tax ban. Five days later, on August 3, the House voted to approve the conference report version by a vote of 328–74. The next day, August 4, the Senate approved the bill by a vote of 79–18.

The final version of the bill, containing a total of nineteen sections, was remarkably similar to that originally submitted to Congress on March 17, 1965. Section 2 strengthened the Fifteenth Amendment by prohibiting acts that denied a citizen the right to vote on the basis of race or color. Section 4 contained the hotly debated trigger, which immediately eliminated literacy or character tests in those places (mostly in the South) where less than 50 percent of those eligible had voted in 1964. A state or district could remove itself from federal supervision if it could demonstrate to the attorney general that it had not used any test or device to prevent blacks from voting in the past five years. To prevent delinquent states (again, mostly in the South) from creating new obstacles to voting, Section 5 required them to submit any new voting requirements to the Justice Department (known as "preclearance") before any changes in voting procedures or redistricting could be approved. Sections 6 through 8 permitted the attorney general to send federal examiners and poll watchers to register voters and supervise elections if necessary. Section 10 stipulated that the payment of a poll tax "precludes persons of limited means from voting," and that therefore "Congress declares that the constitutional right of citizens to vote is denied or abridged . . . by the requirement," and that "the Attorney General is authorized and directed" to bring suit against those four states where the tax still existed (namely, Texas, Alabama, Virginia, and Mississippi). Section 11 made it illegal for any person, "acting under color of law," to intimidate or threaten any person for trying to vote, and Section 12 spelled out the penalties for doing so.

On August 6, 1965, sitting in the President's Room off the Capitol rotunda, President Lyndon B. Johnson signed the Voting Rights Act into law in a nationally televised ceremony. One hundred and three years earlier, President Abraham Lincoln had signed the Emancipation Proclamation in that same room. Poignantly capturing the historic significance of the moment, the president said "This act flows from a clear and simple wrong. Its only purpose is to right that wrong. Millions of Americans are denied the right to vote because of their color. This law will ensure them the right to vote. The wrong is one which no American, in his heart, can justify. The right is one which no American, true to our principles, can deny. . . the vote is the most powerful instrument ever devised by man for breaking down injustice and destroying the terrible walls which imprison men because they are different from other men." Fully aware of the struggles and the resistance that lay ahead, the president continued, "Today, what is perhaps the last of the legal barriers is tumbling. There will be many actions and many difficulties before the rights woven into law are also woven into the fabric of our Nation. But the struggle for equality must now move toward a different battlefield."[16]

Present at the ceremony were Rosa Parks, Dr. King, his chief SCLC lieutenant Reverend Abernathy, and other notables from the civil rights struggle. Interestingly, John Lewis was the only veteran of Bloody Sunday to be present. None of the others who had been brutalized on the bridge that day had been invited, nor were invitations sent to those brave Selma activists, like Amelia Boynton, who had been fighting for voting rights since the 1930s. They would have to take comfort in the knowledge that in spite of all the blood that had been shed, and the lives that had been lost, their efforts to gain the most basic right of citizenship—the right to vote—had not been in vain.

One of the things that the president had emphasized in his speech that day was the need for African Americans to exercise their newly won right. He said, "So let me now say to every Negro in this country: You must register. You must vote. You must learn, so your choice advances your interest and the interest of our beloved Nation. Your future, and your children's future, depend[s] upon it, and I don't believe that you are going to let them down." Admonishing blacks about the importance of voting was one thing; actually getting them to register and vote was quite another. On that morning before the official signing, President Johnson had invited John Lewis, along with a few others, to a private meeting in the Oval Office. As he usually did, the president dominated the conversation, his legs propped on a chair, his large hands folded behind his head. After about twenty minutes, Johnson leaned forward and said, "Now John, you've got to go back and get all those folks registered. You've got to go back and get those boys by the *balls*. Just like a bull gets on top of a cow. You've got to get 'em by the balls and you've got to *squeeze*, squeeze 'em till they *hurt*." Reflecting on that conversation years later, Lewis wrote, "I'd heard that Lyndon Johnson enjoyed talking in graphic, down-home terms, but I wasn't quite prepared for all those bulls and balls."[17]

Despite his less than artful phrasing, the president understood that persistence and organizing would be the key to getting black voters registered, and part of that process included re-educating and re-conditioning older African Americans who had been shut out of the process for so long that they really had come to believe that voting was "white folks business." No one understood this better than the veterans of SNCC, including many of those who had opposed the Selma to Montgomery march from the beginning. But while marching through Lowndes County, many of them seized the opportunity to do some organizing of their own. "We [SNCC] were against the march, I too was against it," remembers Stokely Carmichael, but again, I said it was a *fait accompli*. We couldn't stop it, King was going to have it, and so there was no way to stop it. So all we could do now was to make a positive out of a negative. . . When I entered Lowndes County, I would seek out all of the people from Lowndes County who came to the march. I would get them, write down their names, their addresses, record it, and tell them "Listen, we are going to stay in Lowndes County, we're not just going to pass through," and they would be excited to hear that. So the Black Panther Party was built off of the mobilization that sprouted out of Lowndes County, and he [King] did us a perfect job.[18]

If any blacks were going to be registered in Lowndes County, Alabama, organization and mobilization—and ultimately intervention by the federal government—would be required. In many rural counties in Alabama's Black Belt, blacks outnumbered whites by wide margins, and if this historically disenfranchised population began to vote in significant numbers, nothing short of a political revolution would occur, which helps to explain why white resistance in these areas was so intense. Almost immediately following the passage of the Voting Rights Act, Attorney General Katzenbach and his staff began selecting their first "targets"—areas where they expected stiff resistance to black voting, and where federal registrars would have to be sent. As many as twenty-four counties were initially included on this list, but eventually Katzenbach narrowed his focus to nine counties with the worst record of African American voter suppression: two in Mississippi (Jefferson Davis and Jones), three in Louisiana (East Carroll, Madison, and Ouachita Parishes), and four in Alabama (Dallas, Lowndes, Perry, and Wilcox).[19] Federal examiners were necessary in these places, Katzenbach said, because the evidence was compelling that these designated localities "have continued to discriminate and have given no substantial indication that they will comply with it [the Voting Rights Act]." Hoping to reassure white southerners that this was not going to be a second Reconstruction, with Union soldiers occupying a defeated and divided South, Katzenbach emphasized that this federal intervention would last only as long as necessary. "When local officials demonstrate their willingness to deal fairly with Negro as well as white applicants, the examiners will be withdrawn promptly."[20]

Despite the attorney general's assurances, most southern whites were angry and defiant, convinced that they were about to be subjected to a new era of "Negro rule," such as that depicted in D. W. Griffith's *Birth of a Nation*. Many remained convinced that "their" Negroes were perfectly satisfied with their lot, and that had it not been for a few outside agitators and some determined activists, race relations in the South could have continued much as they always had. But the civil rights movement had changed all that; and now, adding insult to injury, the federal government was inserting itself into affairs that had traditionally been left to the states. Absent from this racial calculus, however, was any acknowledgment from southern whites that, by their own defiance and intransigence, they had largely brought this upon themselves.

The president's ink on the Voting Rights Act had hardly dried before white residents in many southern localities began resisting the new law in a variety of ways. Because the registrars remained all white in the days immediately following the passage of the voting rights bill, the political apparatus remained under white control, and fear and intimidation were legitimate concerns. In an obvious attempt to terrorize and intimidate would-be voters, the Ku Klux Klan in some areas stepped up their nocturnal activities, though they were limited mainly to rallies and a few cross burnings. Local whites also tried to "persuade" their black neighbors that voting was not in their best interests, and since many of these blacks were impoverished sharecroppers who depended upon whites for their economic survival, they were especially vulnerable to intimidation. In the months immediately following the passage of the Voting Rights Act, the eviction rate of black tenants and sharecroppers grew to an alarming level. Civil rights activists in Alabama were so concerned that they filed a complaint with the Justice Department, concluding that "economic intimidation has also increased as a direct result of people registering to vote. . . . In Lowndes, Wilcox, Bullock, and Greene Counties those who have registered have been used as examples. . . . The landowners on the larger plantations will come around to those who have registered to vote and, in front of the rest of the tenants, say 'We just can't use you anymore.' The others . . . quickly get the message."[21]

African Americans who were members of the middle class were not immune from economic intimidation. School teachers, for example, were vulnerable because the public school system that employed them was controlled by an all-white school board. Lawrence Parrish and his wife were two of the first teachers to lose their jobs in Wilcox County, but they were soon joined by fourteen more. And even after the teachers were eventually reinstated following a court order, the school board devised other strategies for punishing them for having registered. In some cases, the board assigned them to schools as far away from their homes as possible, and in cases where both spouses were teachers, husbands and wives were assigned to schools at opposite ends of the county, making it very difficult—if not impossible—for them to get to work on time, especially if they happened to own only one car. Lawrence Parrish became so frustrated that he abandoned teaching for a while and took a job selling real estate.[22]

Yet despite the continued harassment and intimidation they faced, African Americans were determined to add their names to the voting rolls, and they did so in significant numbers. On Tuesday, August 10, the day that federal examiners were scheduled to begin their work, roughly three hundred African Americans lined up to register at the Federal Building in Selma. Some were in their seventies and eighties and had to be physically assisted in order to climb the fifty-two steps to the third floor where examiners were waiting to help them. The registration process was now very different from what it had been, when local white registrars had deliberately set out to *disqualify* black voters rather than qualify them. This time, there was only a form titled "Application to Be Listed under the Voting Rights Act of 1965." Anyone unable to complete the form was asked a series of short questions, such as name, age, address, how long they had lived at their current residence, if they had ever been convicted of a crime, or if they had ever been dishonorably discharged from the armed forces. Once the questions had been answered, the applicant was asked to stand, raise his or her right hand, and swear that the answers given were true, and that he or she would be "well disposed to the good order and happiness of the state of Alabama." Once they answered "I do," the new voters were asked to sign the form (or make their mark) and then they received a "certificate of eligibility to vote."

On that day, Ardies Mauldin, an elderly practical nurse at Selma Hospital, emerged from the Federal Building smiling, having become the first black southerner registered under the Voting Rights Act. "It didn't take but a few minutes," she said. "I don't know why it couldn't have been like that in the first place."[23] By the end of that first day, 107 new voters were registered. Sheriff Jim Clark, wearing his "NEVER" button on his left lapel, was present at the Federal Building that day, but his presence likely evoked more pity than fear, and he made no attempt to interfere with the registration process. Examiners working in the other eight counties in Alabama, Mississippi, and Louisiana recorded 937 new voters, for a first-day total of 1,444. By Friday the number had grown to almost 7,000. By the end of August, figures from the Justice Department showed that nearly 60,000 new black voters had registered in the states of Alabama, Georgia, Louisiana, and Mississippi. Meanwhile, the state of South Carolina was busy petitioning the United States Supreme Court to declare the Voting Rights Act unconstitutional.[24]

It was not necessarily the presence of federal examiners that made the difference in black voter registration in the early days after the passage of the Voting Rights Act, but rather the extent of community organization. No one understood this better than Stokely Carmichael. Born in Trinidad in 1941, Carmichael moved to New York in 1952 to rejoin his parents. A senior at the prestigious Bronx High School of Science when the lunch counter sit-ins began, he became actively involved in civil rights demonstrations. Carmichael helped organize the Student Nonviolent Coordinating Committee in 1960. The following year he participated in the freedom rides which resulted in his spending fifty-three days in Mississippi's notorious Parchman Penitentiary, where guards beat him regularly. In the early sixties, he attended Howard University and with several other students formed the Nonviolent Action Group (NAG), a SNCC affiliate. Heavily influenced by the writings of Karl Marx and the fiery rhetoric of Malcolm X, Carmichael's experiences in the Mississippi Delta and the Alabama Black Belt gradually led to his increasing militancy. In May 1966, the twenty-four-year-old Carmichael replaced John Lewis as chairman of SNCC, signaling a change in direction of the organization from integration toward black nationalism.

Like other young SNCC activists who had been subjected to beatings and abuse from white civilians and law enforcement officials alike, Carmichael was beginning to question his own commitment to nonviolence. During a march near Canton, Mississippi, in 1966, when he was asked whether he was as committed to nonviolence as Dr. King was, he responded, "No I'm not. I just don't see it as a way of life; I never have. I also realize that no one in this country is asking the white community in the South to be nonviolent, and that in a sense is giving them a free license to shoot us at will." The next day, Carmichael would inject a new phrase into the movement designed to draw a sharp contrast between SNCC's new militancy and SCLC's adherence to integration and nonviolence. When peaceful marchers were beaten and tear-gassed by Mississippi state police on the grounds of a black high school in Canton, Carmichael told the crowd, "We don't want anybody to move; the time for running has come to an end. You tell them white folk in Mississippi that all the scared niggers are dead. You tell them they shot all the rabbits, now they got to deal with the men. We need Black Power! What do you want?" The crowd responded enthusiastically, "Black Power!" This new emphasis on "Black Power" would dramatically alter the direction of the freedom struggle, but it would be another year before the civil rights movement would arrive at that particular crossroad.[25]

Capitalizing on the energy and enthusiasm they had created during the march, Carmichael and SNCC launched an intensive effort in Lowndes County that summer to get blacks registered. Going from door to door, Carmichael spearheaded efforts to inform local blacks about the voting process as well as what their rights were under the new voting bill. He also made the point of emphasizing the social revolution that would occur in the South if blacks voted. Eighty-six white families owned 90 percent of the land in the county and controlled the local government. Although 80 percent of Lowndes County's population was black in 1965, there were no black elected officials, and no blacks had been allowed to register. But if Carmichael and SNCC had their way, that would soon change. "Now in this country it says majority rule; and we are 80 percent of this county, and we have a right to rule this county," Carmichael constantly repeated to his black audiences. "We have a right to rule this county. I don't care how poor we are or how black we are, we are going to rule it."[26] Carmichael's efforts led to the creation of the Lowndes County Freedom Organization (LCFO), an independent political party aimed at encouraging blacks to overcome their fear and become involved in the voting process.

John Hulett, a prominent member of LCFO who would go on to become Lowndes County's first elected black sheriff in 1970, remembers the role that SNCC organizers played in educating them about their political rights. "Stokely Carmichael and Courtland Cox told us that if we didn't like what the Democratic Party or the Republican Party was doing in our county, we could form our own political organization." As governor, George Wallace was the head of Alabama's Democratic Party, whose official emblem was a white rooster with a banner over its head proclaiming "White Supremacy." So as to provide a stark contrast with the racist white rooster (and to ensure that illiterate black voters were not confused), LCFO chose a black panther as its political symbol, and hence the Lowndes County Freedom Organization quickly became better known as the "Black Panther Party." Student activist John Jackson recalls that "everybody was excited. We said, well, they have the rooster which represents the Democratic Party, the elephant which represents the Republican Party, why can't we have a black cat to represent us? Everybody knows how a cat looks. And we were excited. Because we knew that if a person couldn't read or write, they sure knew the difference between a cat, an elephant, and a rooster." Throughout the county, activists erected signs and billboards which read, "PULL THE LEVER for the BLACK PANTHER and go HOME!" (When Huey Newton and Bobby Seale created their organization in Oakland, California, in 1966, they appropriated the black panther symbol from the Lowndes County Freedom Organization.)[27]

Blacks' sudden interest in voting angered whites in Lowndes County. Whites refused to serve known LCFO members in stores and restaurants. Economically dependent upon whites, many black tenants and sharecroppers were evicted because they had voted, leaving them homeless. Lowndes County Solicitor Carleton Purdue once said publicly that "We got ways to keep Nigras in their place . . . We have the banks, the credit . . . We could force them to their knees if we so choose."[28] SNCC and LCFO leaders worked to help these families by purchasing tents, cots, heaters, food, and water, and by providing them with a temporary housing facility known as "Tent City." Despite frequent harassment, including shots regularly fired into the encampment, residents persevered for nearly two years as organizers helped them find new jobs and relocate to permanent housing. And while they continued to register, persistent fear was a far greater obstacle than apathy. Blacks in Lowndes County had reason to be afraid: almost half of the lynchings that had occurred in Alabama between 1880 and 1930 had occurred in Lowndes County.

Stokely Carmichael had made a point to emphasize to Lowndes County residents that he, along with other SNCC staffers, planned to remain until such time as the newly created local organization could sustain itself. Another civil rights worker who made a similar commitment was a white, twenty-six-year-old seminary student named Jonathan Daniels. An Episcopal seminarian from Keene, New Hampshire, Daniels had answered Dr. King's call for clergy and all people of good will to come to Selma to take part in the march. Daniels came to Selma intending to stay only until the march concluded in Montgomery, but after missing his bus back to Cambridge he began to have second thoughts about returning home so soon. He requested, and was granted, permission from the Episcopal Theological School in Cambridge, Massachusetts, to spend the rest of the semester working in Selma, with plans to return to school at the end of the term to take his exams.

While in Selma, Daniels stayed with the Wests, a local black family. During the next few months he worked to integrate the local Episcopal Church by taking groups of young blacks to the church. Much to his dismay, the white congregants did not extend a warm welcome to their darker brothers and sisters in Christ. Daniels returned to Cambridge long enough to take his exams before heading back to Alabama to continue his work. He helped assemble a list of federal, state, and local agencies that could provide assistance to those in need, tutored children, and helped with voter registration.

On Friday, August 13, Daniels was one of roughly twenty-five protestors (including several SNCC activists) who traveled to the town of Fort Deposit, Alabama, to participate in a voting rights demonstration and to picket three local businesses that refused to serve blacks. The next day they were all arrested and taken to jail in the nearby town of Hayneville. The five juveniles that were part of the group were released from jail the next day, but the rest of the group was held for six days, all agreeing that none of them would accept release on bail until there was bail money for everyone. After their release on Friday, August 20, Daniels and Richard Morrisroe, a Catholic priest, accompanied two black teenagers, Joyce Bailey and Ruby Sales, to buy a soda at Varner's Cash Store, one of the few local stores to serve blacks. But upon their arrival they were met at the door by Tom Coleman, a white construction worker and part-time deputy sheriff who had arrived at the store only minutes earlier after receiving word that the released civil rights workers were walking the streets.

Wearing a holster with a pistol and holding a twelve-gauge shotgun, Coleman shouted to the integrated group that the store was closed and ordered them "to get off this property, or I'll blow your goddamn heads off, you sons of bitches." When Daniels asked why he was threatening them Coleman aimed his shotgun at seventeen-year-old Ruby Sales. Daniels quickly pushed her out of the way and to the ground as Coleman, standing only a few feet from Daniels, fired his shotgun. Daniels took the full impact of the blast, a load of buckshot tearing a hole in the right side of his chest. He died instantly. At the first shot, Morrisroe grabbed Joyce Bailey's hand and turned to flee, but Coleman aimed his shotgun and fired again. Buckshot struck the priest in the lower right back and side, and he fell to the ground, but he did survive the shooting. The two black girls then ran for safety while Coleman threatened to shoot several other blacks standing on the corner. He then left his shotgun at the store and drove to the county courthouse.[29]

A grand jury indicted Coleman for manslaughter. Alabama Attorney General Richmond Flowers had pushed for a murder indictment, but his argument did not move an unsympathetic judge. Further frustrating the prosecution, Judge T. Werth Thagard refused to delay the trial until Father Morrisroe was well enough to testify, saying that the defendant had a right to a speedy trial. The defense witnesses and the defense attorneys claimed that Daniels and Morrisroe, along with "some nigger women," had gone to the store "looking for trouble," and that Coleman was there trying "to preserve the peace" and had acted "in self-defense." In a reference to Daniels's clerical attire, one of Coleman's attorneys quoted scripture, telling the jurors to "beware of false prophets which come to you in sheep's clothing, for inwardly they are ravening wolves." Raising the specter of interracial sex and racial amalgamation, the same attorney also told the jurors that Daniels had been seen kissing a black woman after he was released from jail and that, therefore Tom Coleman had acted wisely and bravely when he in effect said, "This far shall they come and no further—here all evil must cease." After deliberating for one hour and thirty-one minutes, the all-white jury found Tom Coleman not guilty.[30] Coleman, who had already killed a man several years earlier and whom the *New York Herald-Tribune* had described before the verdict as being "known as a violent, heavy-drinking man, maddened by the prospect of Negroes voting in Lowndes County," continued working as an engineer for the state highway department until his death on June 13, 1997, at the age of eighty-six. He would never face further prosecution.

Jonathan Daniels's murder was further proof that some southern whites would stop at nothing to preserve the old social order that now appeared to be under siege as a result of new voting laws and an energized black community; anyone, black or white, who was perceived to be an agent of change could be killed at any moment. The passage of the Voting Rights Act had removed—at least on paper—the last remaining barriers to African Americans' inclusion in the political process, and blacks wasted little time in testing the limits of their newly won rights. But their political gains often came with a heavy price. Future electoral successes in the black community—at the local, state, and national levels—would require continued organization and mobilization. And while many electoral triumphs would be realized in the years to come, battles that had been fought and presumably won in the 1960s would eventually be played out again as the nation's changing demographics began to alter the political landscape.

Epilogue

THE VOTING RIGHTS ACT OF 1965 dramatically changed the nature of southern politics. White politicians who in the past had taken blacks for granted because they were politically disenfranchised suddenly realized that the system they had fought so desperately to preserve had been transformed overnight. Owing to the strength of a newly empowered black electorate, white politicians would no longer have the luxury of engaging in vicious race-baiting, in which some had previously boasted of the number of times they used the word "nigger" in their campaign speeches. Subtle appeals to race did not disappear, of course, but white politicians were careful to alter their language to be more in line with the new political realities.

White southerners of all political stripes suddenly had to take notice of African American voters, but the task of winning over black voters would obviously be easier for the racial moderates than for the die-hard segregationists. Alabama's attorney general Richmond Flowers would be among the first politicians in the state to make an overt appeal to black voters in his bid to succeed George Wallace as governor in 1966. Best known for his unsuccessful efforts to obtain convictions in Lowndes County of the Klansmen accused of murdering Viola Liuzzo, and of Tom Coleman for the 1965 murder of seminarian Jonathan Daniels, Flowers was very much at ease campaigning in black communities. A Democrat and a racial moderate, Flowers enjoyed widespread support among black voters, and it certainly helped him to have Martin Luther King's support as well as the endorsement of Alabama's two largest black political organizations, the Confederation of Alabama Political Organizations and the Alabama Democratic Conference. If elected, Flowers promised to remove the Confederate flag that flew atop the state capitol as well as remove the words "White Supremacy" from the state's party emblem. He also promised to appoint blacks to positions in his administration, and even joined them in singing "We Shall Overcome."

But just as blacks had registered in record numbers in the days leading up to the primary, so too had whites, virtually all of whom maintained their strong allegiance to Wallace. An aggressive get-out-the-vote campaign by Wallace's staff added 110,000 new white voters to the rolls, thereby decreasing black influence even as the number of black voters increased. Alabama law at the time prevented the governor from succeeding himself, so Wallace could not run for re-election. But there was no prohibition against his wife running for governor. Wallace's wife, Lurleen, was suffering from cancer and had never before sought political office, but none of that mattered to most white Alabamians who were pleased that *any* Wallace was on the ballot (she chose to run not as the former "Lurleen Burns" but as "Mrs. George C. Wallace"). Ignoring criticism that she was only a "proxy" candidate and a "caretaker" of the office until her husband was eligible to run again, Mrs. Wallace kicked off her campaign in Birmingham, pledging "progress without compromise" and "accomplishment without surrender . . . George will continue to speak up and stand up for Alabama."[1] Unlike Flowers, Mrs. Wallace did not seek black political support, and her husband kept the racial issue alive by continuing to resist school desegregation in the state. Mrs. Wallace's campaign slogan, "Two Governors, One Cause," was unambiguous, and she handily won the primary over the moderate Flowers (who received 90 percent of the black vote) and then went on to defeat Republican James Martin in the general election. She won 63.4 percent of the votes and carried all but two counties in Alabama (losing one by only six votes). But despite her husband's persistent lies to the press that his wife had "won the fight" against cancer, Mrs. Wallace's condition deteriorated rapidly. She died on May 7, 1968, at the age of forty-one, having served fewer than sixteen months in office. To date, she remains the only woman to be elected governor of Alabama and is also the only female governor in U.S. history to have died in office.

Even though George Wallace's wife won the governor's race in 1966, political observers were quick to point out that there had been some notable changes in Alabama's political discourse on matters of race. Reporters covering the campaign noted that certain words that had been used in previous speeches and leaflets had disappeared, and one veteran Alabama journalist observed that he had attended a month's worth of rallies without hearing the word "nigger." George Wallace, long accustomed to saying "Nigra," now had to remember the correct pronunciation for "Negro." "Segregation" was replaced with "states' rights" as white southern politicians continued to search for less-offensive euphemisms to convey their intent. "Accomplishment without surrender" did not strike quite the same tone as "segregation forever," but the similarities were such that there was no confusing the meaning.[2]

Richmond Flowers had a track record and a reputation as a racial moderate that could win him support from black voters, but others claiming to have had a Saul-like conversion while on the road to Damascus would face an uphill battle to convince a skeptical black electorate. In his campaign to be elected sheriff of Jefferson County, Al Lingo actively sought black votes, telling a reporter for the *Southern Courier*, "I am not a racist." Director of the Alabama Department of Public Safety from 1963 to 1965 and one of the key players involved in Bloody Sunday, Lingo told a reporter "I have many Negro friends. A lot of good colored people here are actively working for my campaign."[3] As for his involvement in Bloody Sunday, Lingo always maintained that he was only following orders and that he later became the "scapegoat" for everything that happened on the bridge. He promised that if elected, the sheriff's office would include black deputies, but most blacks remained unconvinced. Lingo lost to the incumbent.

Seeking re-election as sheriff of Dallas County in 1966, Jim Clark surely knew that his campaign would make no inroads into the black community, but he tried nonetheless, even removing the "NEVER" button that he had worn on his lapel for years. But that was too little too late, and black votes made the difference in retiring Jim Clark from office permanently in 1966. Veteran activist Fred Shuttlesworth perhaps summed it up best: "A man can't beat us up in 1964 and 1965 and expect us to vote for him in 1966."[4] Clark attempted to have 1,600 votes cast for his opponent, Wilson Baker, disqualified because of "irregularities," but the court allowed the votes to stand. Clark would never again hold public office. In 1978, a federal grand jury in Montgomery indicted him on charges of conspiring to smuggle three tons of marijuana from Colombia. Clark was sentenced to two years in prison and ended up serving nine months. In 2006, he told the *Montgomery Advertiser* that as for his role in opposing voting rights for blacks, "Basically, I'd do the same thing today if I had to do it all over again."[5] Jim Clark died at a nursing facility in Elba, Alabama, on June 4, 2007, from a stroke and a heart condition at the age of eighty-four.

To some extent, the great expectations created by the new voting rights legislation did not always mirror reality. As one observer noted, "the first election under the Voting Rights Act was a preview of the struggles to come over the next forty years. Over the decades, obstruction and intimidation continued, but in more subtle ways."[6] No longer able to keep blacks from voting legally, some white southern politicians began to resort to the same kinds of schemes and subterfuges that had enabled their ancestors to make a mockery of the Fifteenth Amendment for ninety-five years. Offices that were once elective suddenly became appointive, with white incumbents doing the appointing. Running for office also became more expensive. In Lowndes County, for example, the cost of filing for office was raised to $500, an amount high enough to discourage all but the most affluent blacks. Some positions were eliminated while the terms of other offices were extended to keep whites in power. Gerrymandering—the practice of drawing congressional districts in such a way as to dilute minority voting strength—would be a constant problem. Since whites controlled the state legislature, they were able to create political districts that retained a white majority. On a municipal level, cities that became increasingly black over time due to demographic shifts often annexed portions of neighboring white counties in an attempt to maintain a white electoral majority. Further, many city governments while under white control opted to replace *single-member* districts (where candidates ran in specific districts, boosting minority candidates' chances of victory) to *at-large* districts, where all candidates were chosen in a citywide contest, which usually resulted in defeat for all minority candidates if the city was still majority white.

Fear remained a powerful deterrent, and even when blacks voted, they did not always support other blacks. Some black voters openly admitted to being afraid to vote for black candidates—some because of the repercussions that they themselves might face, and some out of concern for what might happen to the candidate. This was the reality that Walter Calhoun faced when he sought to become Wilcox County's first African American sheriff. "It was too early for us to have a colored sheriff," said Leo Taylor, a black house painter and school bus driver. "The white folks wouldn't have liked that a bit and it would have caused us some trouble." Taylor voted for Calhoun's white opponent. A black clergyman told Greene County sheriff candidate Thomas Gilmore, "If I vote for you and you win, they'll kill you. It's a nail in your coffin. I'm not gonna help kill you." Moreover, because many rural blacks remained economically dependent upon white employers, fear combined with economic intimidation meant that a black electoral majority did not always translate into black political victory. For a myriad of reasons, many blacks voted for white candidates even when blacks were on the ballot.[7]

Such challenges notwithstanding, the Voting Rights Act resulted in the re-enfranchisement of most African Americans in the South. Within four years of its passage, roughly 60 percent of blacks in the South were registered, with some of the most significant gains occurring in those areas where resistance to black voting rights had been the most violent. In Mississippi, black registration jumped from 6.7 percent in 1964 to 59.4 in 1968. In Alabama during those same years the black percentage of registered voters grew from 23 percent to 53 percent. In Dallas County, the scene of the Selma demonstrations, the number of registered black voters increased from fewer than 1,000 to more than 8,500 within months of the new law taking effect.[8]

As the number of black registered voters increased, so too did the chances that blacks could be elected to office. Blacks stood the best chances of winning office where they outnumbered whites, primarily at the local level. A decade after passage of the Voting Rights Act nearly 50 percent of black elected officials held municipal government positions, and roughly 60 percent of those were in small towns with a population under 5,000. In larger cities with white majorities, blacks did not fare as well. One of the consequences of increased black voter registration was the massive voter registration drives aimed at increasing the number of white voters, and unless black candidates could win white support, they had little chance of winning office at the state level. And while overt race-baiting had diminished, the darker side of southern politics had by no means disappeared. As one observer noted, although explicit references to race had largely disappeared, "it is the underlying and motivating issue in all contests."[9]

The passage of the Voting Rights Act had far-reaching implications regarding national politics as the electoral map changed almost overnight. The South had been solidly Democrat since the Civil War; but, while southern Democrats on the state and local level had remained largely conservative and still identified with white supremacy, the national Democratic Party had become more progressive over the years, as reflected in the increasing level of support for civil rights in the Truman, Kennedy, and Johnson Administrations. President Johnson expressed concern that the civil rights legislation passed in the 1960s would alienate large numbers of white southerners who had in the past supported national Democratic candidates, and that the Republican Party would soon become a more attractive alternative. Just two months after passage of the Civil Rights Act, life-long segregationist Strom Thurmond, first elected United States Senator from South Carolina in 1956 as a Democrat, switched to the Republican Party on September 16, 1964—a move repeated by many other southern Democrats over the next decade. Thurmond played a significant role in attracting white South Carolinians to the Republican presidential campaigns of Barry Goldwater in 1964 (who openly opposed the Civil Rights Act) and Richard Nixon in 1968 (whose campaign of "law and order" was clearly aimed at white conservative voters who had had enough of civil rights legislation and urban rebellions). Although Goldwater's extremist views did not resonate with most Americans in 1964, Nixon's more subtle appeals to race proved to be a successful strategy when he ran against Hubert Humphrey in 1968. Nixon and George Wallace (who ran as a third party independent) carried every southern state except Texas, Johnson's home state, which Humphrey won by less than two percentage points. By 1968, the handwriting was on the wall: the South, which had been solidly Democratic in past presidential contests, would soon become solidly Republican.[10]

No sooner had Republicans regained control of the presidency than a push began for weakening enforcement of voting rights laws. Originally set to expire in 1970, the Voting Rights Act has been reauthorized periodically and for varying periods of time, with each extension being accompanied by debates over which changes should be made and which parts of the country should be covered under the enforcement provisions. When the Act was up for renewal for the first time in 1970, President Nixon's attorney general John Mitchell attempted to weaken the bill—or perhaps eliminate it entirely—by calling for only a three-year renewal. Additionally, he wanted to eliminate the preclearance provision, which requires states or any areas covered under the Act to submit any voting changes to the Justice Department to be approved in advance—or "precleared"—before the changes could go into effect. Under Mitchell's proposal, the covered areas would not need Justice Department approval for any voting changes; rather, the states would be free to change their voting laws at their leisure, requiring the Justice Department to issue a challenge only *after* the changes had become law. In other words, the burden of proof would shift: the Justice Department would now have to prove that the states were still engaging in racially discriminatory voting practices rather than the states having to prove that they were not.

Enraged by the attorney general's announcement, a group of civil rights activists staged a sit-in at Mitchell's office. The Mitchell Bill set off a firestorm of debate and controversy within the Congress. While it appealed to southern supporters who felt that federal supervision of their elections was like a second Reconstruction, it angered those—including a number of pro–civil rights northern Republicans—who believed it was far too soon to remove federal oversight. After heated debate the bill was eventually defeated, and President Nixon signed the Voting Rights Act extension into law on June 22, 1970. The Voting Rights Act had survived its first renewal test, but the experience provided civil rights activists with a glimpse of what lay ahead. Unlike five years earlier, there was no public ceremony to mark the occasion.[11]

Beginning in the 1980s it became apparent that black voting rights were once again under attack, as the Supreme Court's new conservative majority handed down a string of decisions that limited African Americans' electoral opportunities. In *Mobile v. Bolden* (1980) the Court ruled that because African Americans in Mobile, Alabama, could register and vote freely, the city's at-large election system did not discriminate against them, even if such a system made it more difficult for blacks to be elected to office. The Court held that discriminatory *effects* had to be accompanied by discriminatory *intent*. Justice Potter Stewart wrote that "disproportionate impact alone cannot be decisive, and courts must look to other evidence to support a finding of discriminatory purpose."[12] In several important decisions in the 1990s, the Court held that race could not be a factor in the creation of voting districts. In *Shaw v. Reno* (1993) the Court ruled that North Carolina's congressional redistricting plan (which had created two predominantly black congressional districts out of a total of twelve districts) constituted racial gerrymandering. The white plaintiffs who had challenged the oddly shaped district alleged that they were the victims of racial segregation by virtue of having been excluded from the district. Speaking for the 5–4 majority, Justice Sandra Day O'Connor agreed. She wrote that the configuration of North Carolina's twelfth district was so bizarre on its face that clear racial intent was the only possible explanation.

Calling the district a version of "political apartheid" (a reference to South Africa's system of rigid racial separation), O'Connor condemned "racial classifications of any sort."[13] In a similar case in 1995, the Court ruled in *Miller v. Johnson* that Georgia's eleventh district, represented by Cynthia McKinney, the first black woman elected to Congress from Georgia, was also flawed—not because of the shape of the district, but because race was the predominant factor in determining the configuration of the district. Writing for the majority, Justice Anthony Kennedy determined that race, "for its own sake," could not be tolerated as a criterion in drawing district boundaries. Equal opportunity could never be achieved, Kennedy wrote, "by carving electorates into racial blocs." Dissenting from the majority opinion, Justice Ruth Bader Ginsburg, appointed to the Court by President Bill Clinton in 1993, argued that the Court's rulings in these cases handicapped the very minority group that the Voting Rights Act had been created to protect.[14]

In 2013, the U.S. Supreme Court dealt voting rights activists a far more devastating blow. In *Shelby County, Alabama v. Holder*, the Court ruled 5–4 that the act's coverage formula, Section 4, was no longer valid, and that affected jurisdictions no longer had to submit voting changes to the Justice Department before going into effect. The Court did not strike down Section 5 (preclearance), but without Section 4, no jurisdiction will be subject to Section 5 preclearance unless Congress enacts a new coverage formula, which as of this writing, Congress has not done (and with Republicans in control of both houses of Congress, is unlikely to do anytime in the foreseeable future). Writing for the Court's majority, Chief Justice John Roberts noted the racial progress that has been made since 1965 and asserted that the Voting Rights Act is "based on 40-year-old facts having no logical relationship to the present day." Justice Antonin Scalia, leader of the conservative bloc, concurred, commenting that the Voting Rights Act was nothing more than the "perpetuation of racial entitlement."[15] Not surprisingly, Scalia's African American protégé Clarence Thomas took an even more extreme view, insisting that the entire Voting Rights Act was unconstitutional.

Responding for the minority of four, Justice Ruth Bader Ginsburg acknowledged the progress that African Americans had made, but also pointed out that there was a significant body of evidence suggesting that racial bias in voting continues, and that this Court "errs egregiously" in invalidating Section 4 of the Act. She wrote that battling racial discrimination in voting "resembled battling the Hydra. Whenever one form of voting discrimination was identified and prohibited, others sprang up in its place."[16] And Justice Ginsburg was correct in her assessment. When Congress voted to renew the Voting Rights Act in 2006, it conducted twenty-one hearings over ten months, gathering 12,000 pages of testimony. Most of the voting rights challenges adjudicated in the federal courts as late as 2006 occurred in those jurisdictions covered under Section 4. One prominent voting rights scholar has noted that "In pronouncing a premature end to the ongoing struggle against racial disfranchisement, the chief justice's opinion appeared inspired by a long-standing political agenda."[17] In the 1980s, Roberts had worked in President Reagan's Justice Department and had argued for weakened enforcement of the Voting Rights Act, a position that he brought with him to the Supreme Court. Another legal analyst wrote that Roberts's mission on the Court was "to declare victory in the nation's fight against racial discrimination and then to disable the weapons with which the struggle was won."[18]

Predictably, within hours of the Court's decision, Texas reinstated its photo ID law, which a federal court judge had previously rejected for imposing "strict, unforgiving burdens" on minority voters. Soon thereafter, North Carolina—which now has the dubious distinction of having the most restrictive voting laws in the nation—imposed tougher voter ID laws, reduced the number of days for early voting, eliminated same-day registration, ended pre-registration for 16- and 17-year-olds, and disqualified provisional ballots cast outside of voters' home precincts. Since the midterm elections of 2010, at least thirty-four states have introduced new "voter suppression" laws—sponsored exclusively by Republicans—making it more difficult for minorities, the poor, the elderly, and college students to vote, and twenty-two states have already implemented such laws. And the Republican Party is determined to capitalize on its congressional electoral majority in the pursuit of its conservative agenda. On February 13, 2016, Justice Scalia, the Court's most conservative member since his appointment in 1986, died in his sleep following an afternoon of quail hunting on a ranch in Shafter, Texas. Fearing that the Court's 5-4 conservative majority might be in jeopardy, Republican senators immediately signaled to the White House that they would not even consider voting to confirm Scalia's successor until after the 2016 presidential election, despite the fact that there was nearly a year left in President Obama's term. Without Justice Department oversight, and with a conservative-leaning federal judiciary, Republican-controlled legislatures will continue to have a free hand to restrict access to the ballot.

Half a century has passed since Bloody Sunday, the march from Selma to Montgomery, and the passage of the Voting Rights Act; such significant milestones are deserving of remembrances and reflections. In an interview conducted in 2014, 103-year-old Amelia Boynton Robinson looked back on her long career as a civil rights activist, and her status as Selma, Alabama's, most distinguished resident. As soon as she turned twenty-one in 1932 she registered to vote, without incident she recalls, because this was before Alabama imposed tough new literacy tests. From that moment on, she committed herself to the struggle for voting rights. When her husband, Sam Boynton, died in 1963, she used his memorial service as an opportunity to register new black voters. It was at her request that both SNCC and SCLC brought their national movements to Selma. When asked why she had dedicated her life to achieving voting rights, she answered simply, "A voteless people is a hopeless people."[19] Yet, despite all she had endured, including being assaulted on the Dallas County Courthouse steps by Sheriff Jim Clark and later being brutally beaten on the Edmund Pettus Bridge on Bloody Sunday, she harbored no resentment or bitterness. The past, she said, is what informs us, but it is that "never-ending hope for a brighter tomorrow that should always drive us forward."[20] When her long-time nemesis Jim Clark died in 2007, she attended his funeral. On August 26, 2015, just months after participating in the fiftieth anniversary commemoration of Bloody Sunday, Amelia Boynton Robinson died at the age of 104.

On March 7, 2015, more than 20,000 people gathered at the Edmund Pettus Bridge to commemorate the fiftieth anniversary of Bloody Sunday. Among the many speakers on hand for this historic moment was Attorney General Eric Holder (the first African American to hold that post) who took the opportunity to criticize voting restrictions pursued by Republican lawmakers. The Supreme Court's recent decision was "profoundly flawed," Holder said. "It has been clear in recent years that fair and free access to the franchise is still, in some areas, under siege. Shortly after the historic election of President Barack Obama in 2008, numerous states and jurisdictions attempted to impose rules and laws that had the effect of restricting Americans' opportunities to vote—particularly, and disproportionately, communities of color." Veteran civil rights activist Rev. Jesse Jackson reminded the crowd that "our struggle is not over" and he urged those present to join him in a renewed fight against poverty, which he called "a weapon of mass destruction."[21] And President Obama told the thousands present:

Fifty years from Bloody Sunday, our march is not yet finished. But we are getting closer. The Americans who crossed this bridge were not physically imposing. But they gave courage to millions. They held no elected office. But they led a nation. We gather here to honor the courage of ordinary Americans willing to endure billy clubs and the chastening rod; tear gas and the trampling hoof; men and women who despite the gush of blood and splintered bone would stay true to their North Star and keep marching toward justice.[22]

The historical significance of the nation's first African American president delivering reflections on this occasion could hardly be missed. But this day belonged to John Lewis, one of the most enduring icons of the black freedom struggle. Returning to the place where his skull had been fractured fifty years earlier, Lewis choked back tears as he told those too young to remember:

We come to Selma to be renewed. We come to be inspired. We come to be reminded that we must do the work that justice and equality calls us to do. This city, on the banks of the Alabama River, gave birth to a movement that changed this nation forever. Our country will never, ever be the same because of what happened on this bridge. Some of us were left bloody . . . but we never became bitter. Don't give up on things of great meaning to you. Don't get lost in a sea of despair. Stand up for what you believe. There's still work left to be done. Get out there and push and pull until we redeem the soul of America.[23]

ACKNOWLEDGMENTS

WRITING HISTORY IS USUALLY a solitary undertaking, and certain aspects of the experience of delving deeply into the past are universally shared by all practitioners of the craft. But there was something different, almost emotionally cathartic, about writing this book. Perhaps it was the timing, and the many reflections commemorating the fiftieth anniversary of Bloody Sunday, that helped bring the black freedom struggle into sharper focus; or perhaps it was W.E.B. Du Bois's haunting prophesy—more than a century ago—about the persistence of the "color line." Yet despite this pessimistic continuity, the twenty-first century begins with a rich legacy of struggle and achievement that demonstrates the capacity of ordinary people, in the face of overwhelming adversity, to stand together in the pursuit of justice and human dignity. I hope that this volume will offer a deeper understanding of that struggle, and a greater appreciation for those who were engaged in it.

I am indebted to numerous scholars whose previous works on voting rights greatly influenced and inspired this book. Gary May's *Bending toward Justice: The Voting Rights Act and the Transformation of American Democracy*, David Garrow's *Protest at Selma: Martin Luther King, Jr., and the Voting Rights Act of 1965*, Steven F. Lawson's *Black Ballots: Voting Rights in the South, 1944–1969*, Taylor Branch's *At Canaan's Edge: America in the King Years, 1965–68*, John Lewis's *Walking with the Wind: A Memoir of the Movement*, and Cynthia Griggs Fleming's *In the Shadow of Selma: The Continuing Struggle for Civil Rights in the Rural South* were indispensable. The work of other scholars whose focus is on the civil rights movement more broadly was also useful, and they are listed here alphabetically: Clayborne Carson, John Dittmer, Adam Fairclough, Robert J. Norrell, Charles M. Payne, and Juan Williams. I am equally indebted to those individuals whose oral accounts, either through personal interviews or public lectures, helped add a more personal and authentic dimension to this narrative, and they are listed here alphabetically: Joann Bland, Willie Bolden,

Fred Gray, Bernard Lafayette, John Lewis, Amelia Boynton Robinson, C. T. Vivian, Sheyann Webb-Christburg, and Andrew Young.

I wish to acknowledge my editor, Bob Brugger, who meticulously guided this project from its inception. While never rushing me to the finish line, he always managed to provide the perfect blend of encouragement and gentle prodding at just the right time. Somehow I always knew when he needed to see a chapter. I am especially indebted to my UGA colleague Peter Charles Hoffer, who first suggested that I write a book on Selma's voting rights campaign for this series. Both Bob and Peter read every sentence and offered valuable advice at critical stages of production. For their assistance in helping to guide this project from beginning to end, I am grateful.

Last, but never least, I reserve my greatest expression of love and gratitude for my wife, Anita, and our two children, Raven and Steven. May they live long enough to witness a society where all barriers to voting are removed once and for all and where the right to participate freely in our cherished democracy is not frustrated, but encouraged.

NOTES

Prologue

1. John Lewis, *Walking with the Wind: A Memoir of the Movement* (New York: Simon and Schuster, 1998), 338–39.

2. Ibid., 339.

CHAPTER ONE: Slow March toward Freedom

Epigraph: Quoted in Nell Irvin Painter, *Creating Black Americans: African-American History and Its Meanings, 1619 to the Present* (Oxford: Oxford University Press, 2007), 148.

1. *Dred Scott v. Sandford*, 60 U.S. 393 (1857).

2. Under the terms of General Sherman's Field Order 15, the freedmen were not actually given the land, but were given "possessory titles," which meant that they might indeed be eligible for permanent ownership at some future date. President Johnson's pardons returning ownership of the land to the former Confederates ended that possibility.

3. Convict leasing was the system wherein blacks convicted of minor offenses would be sentenced to long terms as convicts and then leased out to local landowners, who exploited their labor. Unlike slave owners, who had a financial interest in their slave property, landowners had nothing invested in the convicts, leading to widespread exploitation and physical abuse.

4. Painter, *Creating Black Americans*, 148.

5. Ibid. See also Deborah Gray White, Mia Bay, and Waldo Martin, *Freedom on My Mind: A History of African Americans* (Boston: Bedford / St. Martin's Press, 2013), 391–93.

6. For a fuller discussion of black representation in Congress, see William L. Clay, *Just Permanent Interests: Black Americans in Congress, 1870–1991* (New York: Penguin, 1992).

7. In the disputed presidential election of 1876, the Democrat Samuel J. Tilden had more popular votes than the Republican candidate Rutherford B. Hayes. Tilden also led in the Electoral College, but was one vote short of the number needed to secure the presidency. Twenty electoral votes were being disputed in the states of Oregon, South Carolina, Louisiana, and Florida. When a special electoral commission awarded all twenty disputed votes to Hayes—Hayes needed all twenty to win

the presidency, Tilden only needed one—southern Democrats were furious. In the "Compromise of 1877," Republican Party leaders agreed to certain concessions made to the Democrats in exchange for their acceptance of the decision rendered by the commission. One of those concessions was to remove the last of the federal troops from the South.

8. Quoted in the transcript of *The Rise and Fall of Jim Crow*, episode 2, "Fighting Back, 1896–1917" (PBS, 2002).

9. Ibid.

10. Quoted in Clay, *Just Permanent Interests*, 42.

11. Julien C. Monnet, "The Latest Phase of Negro Disfranchisement," *Harvard Law Review* 26, no. 1 (Nov. 1912), 42. See also Richard H. Pildes, "Democracy, Anti-Democracy, and the Canon," *Constitutional Commentary* 17 (2000), 19–20.

12. See Patricia Sullivan, *Lift Every Voice: The NAACP and the Making of the Civil Rights Movement* (New York: New Press, 2009).

13. See Steven F. Lawson, *Black Ballots: Voting Rights in the South, 1944–1969* (New York: Columbia University Press, 1976), 87–88.

14. Ibid., 134. See also Darlene Clark Hine, *Black Victory: The Rise and Fall of the White Primary in Texas* (Millwood, New York: KTO Press, 1979).

15. Quoted in Lawson, *Black Ballots*, 102.

16. Ibid., 100.

17. Ibid., 103.

18. Ibid., 132.

19. See Charles Payne, *I've Got the Light of Freedom: The Organizing Tradition and the Mississippi Freedom Struggle* (Berkeley and Los Angeles: University of California Press, 1995), 34–35.

20. Legal scholar Michael J. Klarman has been among the leading proponents of the "backlash thesis." See his article, "How *Brown* Changed Race Relations: The Backlash Thesis," *Journal of American History* (June 1994), 81–118.

21. One of the most important voting rights victories during this period was *Gomillion v. Lightfoot*, 364 U.S. 339 (1960), in which the U.S. Supreme Court ruled that electoral districts created in Tuskegee, Alabama, which disenfranchised blacks violated the Fifteenth Amendment. See Robert J. Norrell, *Reaping the Whirlwind: The Civil Rights Movement in Tuskegee* (New York: Alfred A. Knopf, 1985).

22. Juan Williams, *Eyes on the Prize: America's Civil Rights Years, 1954–1965* (New York: Viking Penguin, 1987), 226.

23. Ibid., 226–28.

24. Ibid., 232.

25. Ibid., 235.

CHAPTER TWO: Seeds of Protest

Epigraph: Interview with Albert Turner, conducted by Blackside, Inc., in 1979, for *Eyes on the Prize: America's Civil Rights Years (1954–1965)*. Washington University

Libraries, Film and Media Archive, Henry Hampton Collection. These transcripts contain material that did not appear in the final program.

1. See Cynthia Griggs Fleming, *In the Shadow of Selma: The Continuing Struggle for Civil Rights in the Rural South* (Lanham, MD: Rowman and Littlefield, 2004), 141–43. See also *Andrew Young Presents*, "Leaving Selma" (Smokerise Entertainment, 2011), interview with Bernard Lafayette.

2. Juan Williams, *Eyes on the Prize: America's Civil Rights Years, 1954–1965* (New York: Penguin Books, 1987), 252–53.

3. Ibid., 254.

4. Ibid., 255.

5. See David Garrow, *Protest at Selma: Martin Luther King, Jr., and the Voting Rights Act of 1965* (New Haven: Yale University Press, 1978), 33–34.

6. Williams, *Eyes on the Prize*, 255.

7. Comments by Andrew Young, delivered at the Annual Martin Luther King, Jr., Freedom Breakfast, January 23, 2015, at the University of Georgia.

8. Williams, *Eyes on the Prize*, 255, 258.

9. Garrow, *Protest at Selma*, 39.

10. Williams, *Eyes on the Prize*, 258.

11. Garrow, *Protest at Selma*, 43.

12. Ibid.

13. Williams, *Eyes on the Prize*, 259–60; quoted in the transcript of *Eyes on the Prize*, episode 6, "Bridge to Freedom (1965)" (Blackside/PBS, 1987).

14. *Eyes on the Prize*, episode 6, "Bridge to Freedom"; Williams, *Eyes on the Prize*, 260.

15. Williams, *Eyes on the Prize*, 260.

16. Garrow, *Protest at Selma*, 47.

17. Ibid., 49.

18. Williams, *Eyes on the Prize*, 262.

19. For a more detailed treatment of Malcolm X, see Manning Marable, *Malcolm X: A Life of Reinvention* (New York: Viking, 2011).

20. Bernard Lafayette, Jr., and Kathryn Lee Johnson, *In Peace and Freedom: My Journey in Selma* (Lexington: University of Kentucky Press, 2013), 112–18.

21. Garrow, *Protest at Selma*, 51–52.

22. Martin Luther King, Jr., "A Letter from a Selma, Alabama, Jail," *New York Times*, February 5, 1964, 15.

23. Garrow, *Protest at Selma*, 56.

24. Ibid., 57.

25. Ibid., 57–58.

26. Ibid., 58–59.

27. Williams, *Eyes on the Prize*, 264.

28. Ibid., 265.

29. Ibid.; *Eyes on the Prize*, episode 6, "Bridge to Freedom."

30. Williams, *Eyes on the Prize*, 271.

31. *Andrew Young Presents*, "Leaving Selma."

32. Lafayette and Johnson, *In Peace and Freedom*, 120.

33. See also *Andrew Young Presents*, "Leaving Selma."

34. Williams, *Eyes on the Prize*, 267; *Eyes on the Prize*, episode 6, "Bridge to Freedom."

35. Lafayette and Johnson, *In Peace and Freedom*, 121–22.

36. Ibid., 122.

CHAPTER THREE: Bloody Sunday

Epigraph: Personal interview with Joanne Bland, July 18, 2008, Selma, Alabama.

1. David Garrow, *Protest at Selma: Martin Luther King, Jr., and the Voting Rights Act of 1965* (New Haven: Yale University Press, 1978), 66–67.

2. Juan Williams, *Eyes on the Prize: America's Civil Rights Years, 1954–1965* (New York: Penguin Books, 1987), 267.

3. Garrow, *Protest at Selma*, 68.

4. John Lewis with Michael D'Orso, *Walking with the Wind: A Memoir of the Movement* (New York: Simon and Schuster, 1998), 330.

5. Garrow, *Protest at Selma*, 70.

6. For a detailed discussion of this proposal, see ibid., 70–72.

7. Quoted in the transcript of *Eyes on the Prize*, episode 6, "Bridge to Freedom (1965)" (Blackside/PBS, 1987).

8. See Williams, *Eyes on the Prize*, 268–69.

9. Ibid.

10. See Bernard Lafayette, Jr., and Kathryn Lee Johnson, *In Peace and Freedom: My Journey in Selma* (Lexington: University of Kentucky Press, 2013), 123.

11. King's own account appears in "Behind the Selma March," *Saturday Review* 48 (3 April 1965): 16–17, 57. See also Paul Good, "Beyond the Bridge," *Reporter* 32 (8 April 1965): 23–26, and Jim Bishop, *The Days of Martin Luther King, Jr.* (New York: Putnam, 1971), 385, all quoted in Garrow, *Protest at Selma*, 271, n. 82.

12. See Lewis, *Walking with the Wind*, 336.

13. Ibid., 337.

14. Ibid., 338–39.

15. Ibid., 339.

16. Lafayette and Johnson, *In Peace and Freedom*, 125; Lewis, *Walking with the Wind*, 339–40.

17. Quoted in Lewis, *Walking with the Wind*, 340–41.

18. Ibid., 340–42.

19. Interview with Joanne Bland, July 18, 2008, Selma, Alabama.

20. Williams, *Eyes on the Prize*, 269, 273.

21. Ibid., 273; Lewis, *Walking with the Wind*, 344.

22. Lewis, *Walking with the Wind*, 342.

23. Ibid., 341–43, and Garrow, *Protest at Selma*, 75–76.

24. Ibid.

25. Lewis, *Walking with the Wind*, 343–44.

26. Ibid., 344–45.

CHAPTER FOUR: My Feets is tired, but my Soul is rested

1. Juan Williams, *Eyes on the Prize: America's Civil Rights Years, 1954–1965* (New York: Viking Penguin, 1987), 273.

2. David Garrow, *Protest at Selma: Martin Luther King, Jr., and the Voting Rights Act of 1965* (New Haven: Yale University Press, 1978), 81–82; quoted in the transcript of *Eyes on the Prize*, episode 6, "Bridge to Freedom (1965)" (Blackside/PBS, 1987).

3. See Gary May, *Bending toward Justice: The Voting Rights Act and the Transformation of American Democracy* (Durham: Duke University Press, 2015), 99, 100.

4. Garrow, *Protest at Selma*, 85–86.

5. May, *Bending toward Justice*, 102.

6. Quoted in Williams, *Eyes on the Prize*, 274, and John Lewis with Michael D'Orso, *Walking with the Wind: A Memoir of the Movement* (New York: Simon and Schuster, 1998), 348.

7. Transcript, *Eyes on the Prize*, episode 6, "Bridge to Freedom."

8. Williams, *Eyes on the Prize*, 275; May, *Bending toward Justice*, 105; transcript from *Eyes on the Prize*, episode six, "Bridge to Freedom."

9. Quoted in Jack Bass, *Taming the Storm: The Life and Times of Judge Frank M. Johnson, Jr., and the South's Fight over Civil Rights* (New York: Doubleday, 1993), 363.

10. May, *Bending toward Justice*, 106.

11. Transcript from *Eyes on the Prize*, episode six, "Bridge to Freedom."

12. May, *Bending toward Justice*, 109.

13. Ibid.

14. Ibid., 110.

15. This exchange between Johnson and Wallace is recounted in ibid., 112–14.

16. Ibid., 114.

17. Ibid., 115.

18. Ibid.

19. President Lyndon B. Johnson, Address to Joint Session of Congress, March 15, 1965.

20. May, *Bending toward Justice*, 120–21.

21. Williams, *Eyes on the Prize*, 278.

22. Lewis, *Walking with the Wind*, 354.

23. Williams, *Eyes on the Prize*, 279.

24. May, *Bending toward Justice*, 130.

25. Ibid.

26. Lewis, *Walking with the Wind*, 356.

27. Ibid., 357.

28. Transcript, *Eyes on the Prize*, episode 6, "Bridge to Freedom."

29. Lewis, *Walking with the Wind*, 357; May, *Bending toward Justice*, 131.

30. May, *Bending toward Justice*, 133–34.

31. Lewis, *Walking with the Wind*, 358.

32. See David Garrow, *Bearing the Cross: Martin Luther King, Jr., and the Southern Christian Leadership Conference* (New York: Random House, 1986), 412.

33. Lewis, *Walking with the Wind*, 360.

34. Transcript from *Eyes on the Prize*, episode six, "Bridge to Freedom." See also Andrew Young, *An Easy Burden: The Civil Rights Movement and the Transformation of America* (New York: HarperCollins, 1996), 366.

35. Transcript, *Eyes on the Prize*, episode 6, "Bridge to Freedom."

CHAPTER FIVE: A Season of Suffering

Epigraph: See J. L. Chestnut, Jr., and Julia Cass, *Black in Selma: The Uncommon Life of J. L. Chestnut, Jr.* (New York: Farrar, Straus, and Giroux, 1990), 201.

1. Gary May, *Bending toward Justice: The Voting Rights Act and the Transformation of American Democracy* (Durham: Duke University Press, 2015), 144.

2. See Taylor Branch, *At Canaan's Edge: America in the King Years, 1965–68* (New York: Simon & Schuster, 2006).

3. May, *Bending toward Justice*, 145.

4. Ibid.

5. Juan Williams, *Eyes on the Prize: America's Civil Rights Years, 1954–1965* (New York: Viking Penguin, 1987), 285.

6. David Garrow, *Bearing the Cross: Martin Luther King, Jr., and the Southern Christian Leadership Conference* (New York: Random House, 1986), 413.

7. See Gary May, *The Informant: The FBI, the Ku Klux Klan, and the Murder of Viola Liuzzo* (New Haven: Yale University Press, 2005).

8. Ibid., 146.

9. Ibid., 150; Transcript from *Eyes on the Prize*, episode 2, "Fighting Back (1957–1962)."

10. May, *The Informant*, 150.

11. Ibid., 151.

12. Ibid., 163.

13. Garrow, *Bearing the Cross*, 128–29; May, *Bending toward Justice*, 162–65.

14. May, *Bending toward Justice*, 165.

15. Ibid., 167. The Twenty-Fourth Amendment to the United States Constitution, ratified in 1964, abolished the use of the poll tax (or any other tax) as a pre-condition for voting in federal elections, but made no mention of poll taxes in state elections. In the 1966 case of *Harper v. Virginia Board of Elections*, the Supreme Court extended the prohibition of poll taxes to state elections. It declared that the imposition of a poll tax in state elections violated the "Equal Protection Clause" of the Fourteenth Amendment to the United States Constitution. The *Harper* ruling was one of several that relied on the Equal Protection Clause of the Fourteenth Amendment rather than the more direct provision of the Fifteenth Amendment. In a two-month period in the spring of 1966, federal courts declared unconstitutional poll tax laws in the last four states that still had them, starting with Texas on February 9. Decisions followed for

Alabama (March 3) and Virginia (March 25). Mississippi's poll tax was the last to fall, declared unconstitutional on April 8, 1966.

16. Comments by President Lyndon B. Johnson, on the signing of the 1965 Voting Rights Act, August 6, 1965.

17. John Lewis with Michael D'Orso, *Walking with the Wind: A Memoir of the Movement* (New York: Simon and Schuster, 1998), 361.

18. Transcript from *Eyes on the Prize II*, episode 1, "The Time Has Come (1964–66)" (Blackside/PBS, 1990).

19. See Frederick D. Wright, "The Voting Rights Act and Louisiana: Twenty Years of Enforcement," *Journal of Federalism* 16 (Fall 1986), 101.

20. Cynthia Griggs Fleming, *In the Shadow of Selma: The Continuing Struggle for Civil Rights in the Rural South* (Lanham, MD: Rowman and Littlefield, 2004), 174.

21. Ibid., 175–76.

22. Ibid., 177.

23. May, *Bending toward Justice*, 173–74.

24. Ibid., 173–76.

25. Transcript from *Eyes on the Prize II*, episode 1, "The Time Has Come."

26. Ibid.

27. Ibid.

28. May, *Bending toward Justice*, 179.

29. Charles W. Eagles, *Outside Agitator: Jon Daniels and the Civil Rights Movement in Alabama* (Chapel Hill: University of North Carolina Press, 1993), 179.

30. Ibid., 236–43.

Epilogue

1. *The Montgomery Advertiser*, September 30, 1966.

2. Gary May, *Bending toward Justice: The Voting Rights Act and the Transformation of American Democracy* (Durham: Duke University Press, 2015), 183.

3. Ibid., 182.

4. Ibid.

5. "Jim Clark, Sheriff Who Enforced Segregation, Dies at 84," *New York Times*, June 7, 2007.

6. May, *Bending toward Justice*, 191.

7. Ibid., 187–88.

8. See Steven F. Lawson, *Running for Freedom: Civil Rights and Black Politics in America since 1941*, 4th ed. (Malden, MA: Wiley Blackwell, 2015), 118.

9. David Garrow, *Protest at Selma: Martin Luther King, Jr., and the Voting Rights Act of 1965* (New Haven: Yale University Press, 1978), 189.

10. The only exceptions to the Republican Party's dominance in the South in presidential contests were in 1976, when Georgia governor Jimmy Carter won every southern state except Virginia, and in 1992 and 1996, when Arkansas governor Bill Clinton ran successfully for the presidency. In 1992, Clinton won Arkansas, Georgia,

Kentucky, Louisiana, and Tennessee. In 1996, he won Arkansas, Florida, Kentucky, Louisiana, and Tennessee.

11. May, *Bending toward Justice*, 204–8.

12. *Mobile v. Bolden*, 446 U.S. 55 (1980).

13. *Shaw v. Reno*, 509 U.S. 630 (1993).

14. *Miller v. Johnson*, 515 U.S. 900 (1995).

15. *Shelby County v. Holder* 570 U.S.___(2013).

16. Ibid.

17. Lawson, *Running for Freedom*, 384–85.

18. Ibid.

19. *Andrew Young Presents*, "Leaving Selma" (Smokerise Entertainment, 2011).

20. Ibid.

21. Comments delivered at the Fiftieth Anniversary Commemoration of Bloody Sunday, Selma, Alabama, March 7, 2015.

22. Ibid.

23. Ibid.

INDEX

Italic page numbers indicate illustrations.